Thoughts about Donna

"An inspiration for those working with victims of childhood trauma." *Changes Magazine.*

"Donna Friess turned her hurt into a halo, her scars into stars, what an inspiration she is to all!!!" Rev. Robert Schuller, Founder of Crystal Cathedral, national figure in television ministry.

Oprah Winfrey introduced Donna Friess and previewed her story on *The Oprah Winfrey Show* stating, "This is a story of power and unbelievable perversion…It was the cover story in the *Los Angeles Times Magazine.* This is a show you cannot afford not to watch!" Oprah Winfrey, television celebrity and social activist.

"A real contribution to women everywhere." *Changes Magazine.*

"It is a wonderful book!" Marilyn Van Derbur, Former Miss America, incest survivor.

"I couldn't put it down. It is inspirational!" *Alpha Gamma Delta International Quarterly*

"It is a gripping story…it keeps the reader moving." U.S. International University *Envoy.*

"A must read for everyone. One of the most important books available. It gives hope. Donna's life story is a beacon of hope and happiness for adult survivors of sexual abuse." Claire Reeves, Founder, Mothers Against Sexual Abuse.

"Cry the Darkness is my most valued possession." Gina, Incest survivor and AIDS patient.

"It changed my life and gave me hope." Sonja, Incest survivor.

"I learned that I was not alone." Lydia, Mother whose daughter was an incest victim.

"Dr. Donna Friess has utilized a horrible childhood life experience and family tragedy as her driving force to help the nation's incest victims. Dr. Friess is a friend and advisor to hundreds of victims and students. She is an inspiration to thousands, a wonderful fun-loving motivational speaker who enjoys surfing and playing with her grandchldren. I am very proud and fortunate to call Donna Friess my friend." Collene Thompson Campbell, Former Mayor, San Juan Capistrano, National Institute of Corrections, Appointed by the U.S. Attorney General.

"Dr. Donna helped to save me from feeling like an invisible piece of nothing. Now I know and feel that I deserve to live and move forward to a fulfilling life. I just love her!!!" Ginni, Coaching client.

"Dr. Donna Friess is the most inspirational person I have ever met. She imparts a divine influence on the mind and soul." Jack H., Former student, certificated drug and alcohol counselor.

"Dr. Friess is very spiritual and life changing." Elizabeth W., Single-mom.

"Daddy's Girls" – Subject of cover story for the *Los Angeles Times Magazine*. Lynn Smith, August 4, 1991.

"Out of Darkness- It took Donna Friess of San Juan Capistrano Decades to Reveal Her Real-life Story of the Tragedy of Incest," *Los Angeles Times,* Dennis McLellen, May 6, 1993.

"Dr. Friess is as beautiful on the inside as the outside." Lea M., Abuse victim, single mom.

"Tarer I morket." Best selling non-fiction book in the history of Egmont (Virkelightedens Verden) publishing, Norway, 1990's. Egmont Bogklub.

"It is with sincere gratitude, that I thank Donna for opening the door and letting some sunshine into our dejected group of women. Her caring, therapeutic style enabled us, as a group, to exhale and feel human at a time when we were bereft. She succeeded in reinstating hope by making us feel a part of the whole. We still have work to do but our inertia is interrupted and she is responsible for that." Gayleen W., Participant, Transitional Makeover Program , Womansage, 2013

Other Books by Donna Friess

Circle of Love: A Guide to Successful Relationships,
3rd Edition

One Hundred Years of Weesha: Centennial 2010

Whispering Waters: Historic Weesha and the Settling
of Southern California
With Janet Tonkovich

A Chronicle of Historic Weesha and the Upper Santa
Ana River Valley
With Janet Tonkovich

Just Between Us: Guide to Healing (out of print)

True Animal Short Stories for Children:

Oh What a Big Surprise!
Three Little Kittens Lost in the Woodpile
Zoe's First Birthday
There's Something Scary in the Shed
Starving in the Woods
Winning the Horse Race
Jessica the Seal

CRY THE DARKNESS
One Woman's Triumph Over
The Tragedy of Incest

Donna L. Friess, Ph.D.
New Foreword by the Author

Hurt Into Happiness Publishing 2013
San Juan Capistrano, California

Library of Congress-in-Publication Data
All Rights Reserved
Copyright 1993 Donna L. Friess

Friess, Donna L.
Cry the darkness: one woman's triumph over the tragedy of
Incest/
Donna L. Friess; with foreword by Susan Forward
Includes bibliographical references.

First printing 1993 by Health Communications, Inc.
3201 S. W. 15th Street, Deerfield Beach, Fl. 33442-8190

1. Friess, Donna L. 2. Incest victims – United States - biography.
3. Adult child sexual abuse victims – United States – biography

Second Printing (Expanded edition) Hurt Into Happiness
Publishing 2013
ISBN-13 978-0-9815767-1-8
ISBN-10 0981576710
32332 Camino Capistrano, Suite 102, San Juan Capistrano, CA
92675

Visit: **www.drdonnafriess.com** and
www.yourtimenow.org to order books

Dedication

For my husband Ken,
my partner,
my soul mate.

Acknowledgments 2013

My husband Ken, as always, is a driving force of encouragement for all my projects. I appreciate him with all my heart. My sister Diana Starr has been an invaluable technical facilitator to this printing as well as the cover designer. Her loving emotional support has also been greatly appreciated.

Acknowledgments 1993

Life's journey sometimes surprises us. One of the most incredible discoveries for me was that the many people in my life – friends, relatives, colleagues and students at Cypress College, my fellow scholars at United States International University and my neighbors in San Juan Capistrano – did not run away from me when they learned of my secret. Quite the contrary, I felt protected and accepted by them all. It shocked me to be cared for by so many dear people. You made this book possible, and I want to thank all of you. You helped hold me together through a difficult time.

Without the daily encouragement from my husband, Ken, when the pain of remembering was overwhelming, and without his intelligent critical thinking, the manuscript might never have been completed. My three children, Rick, Julina and Dan, provided a framework of strength from which I have drawn. I want to acknowledge Leanne and Ron Anteau whose friendship sustained me.

I want to thank the staff at the *Los Angeles Times* for their sensitivity and courage in reporting the story, and especially Lynn Smith, Donna Frazier and John Archer. Bill Penzin and Jim Brown played special roles in this effort. Peter Vegso and Gary Seidler, founders of Health Communications, had the faith to make the project a reality and Barbara Nichols had the editing skills.

There have been many brilliant minds who have influenced my life. I want to acknowledge my appreciation to them for sharing their wisdom with me, especially Susan Forward, Sylvia Lane, Darryl Freeland, Herbert Baker, Alice Miller, Mary Catherine Bateson, Maya Angelou, Oprah Winfrey, John Bradshaw, M. Scott Peck, and Eric Berne.

Lastly, I want to pay tribute to all my brave and beautiful brothers and sisters, nieces and nephews, sisters-and brothers-in-law, who stood tall and resolute. I love you all.

Introduction

The tricky part of the human journey is to transform ourselves continually as our life directions change. Erich Fromm says that we are in the constant process of giving birth to ourselves. We do it from childhood, through the challenges of puberty, adulthood, parenthood and, if we are lucky, old age. Re-creating ourselves is a lifetime effort.

Today life is moving faster than it ever has before, forcing us to alter our courses frequently or risk being lost at sea. We must use our imaginations to improvise new ways of being. I hope we will make decisions with the knowledge that we have the power and freedom to choose lives that are rich and full. Then we will truly become the captains of our ships.

My wish is that by sharing myself with you, you will come away with another perspective on the human condition and will understand better what happens to so many of us and our children at home. There is great strength in self-knowledge.

In the most personal sense, we are defined by our decisions, and, as a people, we are delineated, in part, by how we treat each other. My dream is that as you live out your own life, you will make conscious choices to make our world a better, more gentle place, that you will act to protect the children, all of our children, for they are our hope for the future.

Foreword 2013

Donna L. Friess, Ph.D.

A Life of its Own

Twenty-some years ago, as I dared to write my story, I only hoped that perhaps my children could know me better. As a result, my children do know me better, but the amazing fact to me is that *Cry the Darkness* is its own thing. It has a life of its own quite separate from mine. It is used as a resource by psychologists, school counselors, drug and alcohol case workers, personnel in sanctuaries for women victims of domestic violence and teachers. It is a reference for those within the judicial and law enforcement systems, but mostly I have learned that it has helped other victims such as myself and my sisters. I recently opened a letter from a lady who had read it 18 years ago. She told me that it had changed her life, that she no longer felt alone. Another woman wrote to me that she has owned *Cry the Darkness* for 10 years and has just lately had the courage to read it. It has given her strength. Across the years, I have also received emails from girls and women in other countries. A girl in Norway, for example, read my book as part of her class assignment. She told me that the same thing had happened to her and that since reading it she felt determined enough to seek professional help.

The idea of writing my story came from the detective who worked our case. I still hear his words, "Donna in 20 years of working sex crimes, I have never encountered a case as heinous as this one. You must write a book about it." I recall the drive home that day. My husband, Ken, agreed with the detective. "Donna you should write it." I was very hesitant and presented many counter-arguments, mainly, I had no idea how to write a book, had never considered writing a book, and certainly had no ideas about sharing my awful secret with the world. But a few weeks later, when Ken was out of town, I sat down and began to tell my truth. By the end of that summer I had written 600 pages. Before long it was published in 7 languages and began to take on its own independent existence.

I feel proud that I have contributed to the body of work that sheds light on this all-too-frequent crime against children. On a personal level, since the writing of *Cry the Darkness*, I have somehow felt lighter, freer, that the bad stuff is inside the computer, or within the covers of the book, that it is no longer buried inside of me. If this story has helped one person to know that they are not alone, that there is hope, then I believe that my mission has been accomplished.

Foreword 1993

Susan Forward, Ph.D.

Susan Forward, Ph.D., is an internationally renowned therapist, lecturer and author of several books, including the *New York Times* bestsellers, *Toxic Parents* and *Men Who Hate Women and the Women Who Love Them*. In addition to her private practice, she hosted a daily radio talk show for five years. A pioneer in the field, Dr. Forward formed the first private sexual abuse treatment centers in California.

Incest is the most devastating betrayal a child can endure. It is perhaps the cruelest, most baffling of human experiences. It is a violation of the most basic trust between child and parent or caretaker. These children have nowhere to run, no one to run to. The child is caught as a hostage by a powerful terrorist. The protector becomes the persecutor and reality becomes a prison of dirty secrets. It is estimated that there are 60 million adult victims of childhood sexual abuse in America today.

A little child who has to keep a secret cannot imagine that the big person, the parent, is doing anything wrong. The child survives by turning the feeling of badness inward; their world is orchestrated around this core feeling of shame. Every adult who was molested as a child brings from childhood pervasive feelings of being hopelessly inadequate. All adult victims of incest share a legacy of tragic feelings: they feel Dirty, Damaged and Different – the Three Ds.

Incest leads to a form of psychological cancer. It is usually not terminal, but treatment is necessary and sometimes painful. This is not something that gets better by itself.

There is hope. When the secret of incest is exposed to the light of day and the victims are made to see that the shame is not theirs, they have a chance to stand up and hold their heads high. They have an opportunity to put their past behind them and to make their lives work. They can learn to rebuild their lives and their self-images and can develop a new dignity and sense of personal value. They can learn to lead happy, productive lives. With *Cry The Darkness*, Donna Friess tells the story of her incredible struggle to expose the dark evil of incest to the light of truth. It was a war to save her four-year-old niece's life and the lives of the children dwelling in the adult victims of her father's tyranny. I applaud her courage and her strength.

The names in this book have been changed to protect the privacy of the persons in the story. True names were used only with permission.

Family Members

Raymond Landis, Sr. (Big Ray) – Donna's grandfather

Vera-May Landis (Maymie) – Donna's grandmother

Raymond Landis, Jr. – Donna's father and father of Sandy, Cee Cee, Trey, Chad, Diedre and Connie

Cecelia Burwick Landis – Donna and Sandy's mother, Ray Jr.'s first wife

Sandy – Donna's full younger sister

Bernice Landis – Raymond Landis, Jr.'s second wife, mother of Cee Cee, Trey, Chad, Diedre and Connie

Cee Cee Landis – Donna's oldest half-sister

Trey Landis – Donna's oldest half-brother

Chadwick Landis – Donna's half-brother

Connie Landis – Donna's half-sister

Diedre Landis – Donna's youngest half-sister

Anne Landis – Cee Cee's firstborn daughter

Jesse – Cee Cee's oldest son

Russ – Cee Cee's son

Nick – Cee Cee's son

Keely – Cee Cee's youngest daughter

Kyle – Cee Cee's baby boy

Rand – Cee Cee's 2nd husband

Crystal – Ray Landis, Jr.'s third wife and mother of step-daughter, Jaime

Ken Friess – Donna's husband

Donna and Ken's children: Rick, Julie and Daniel

Sandy's two children: Joanne and Mindy

Prologue

January 18, 1990
Municipal Court
West Los Angeles

I couldn't watch when they brought him into the courtroom in shackles, but I know I'll hear the sound of those chains for the rest of my life. How could I bear seeing my father restrained like some mad dog?

I was torn between the desire to run over and unlock those cruel handcuffs and hug my dad and the need to sit still while legal wheels turned to send him away to prison, maybe for the rest of his life. Breathless with anxiety, I finally mustered the courage to glance up at him. Plastic surgery had left his eyes pulled up into a peculiar slant that made him seem inhuman, demonic, and he looked like an aged satyr glaring at me with icy fury. The full force of his riveting blue eyes went through me like a sword.

I was terrified. My heart pounded in my chest and the agony I felt shook me to my soul. A small voice inside was crying out, "I love you, Daddy. How will I ever live without your love?"

The four-year-old voice within was drowned out by the threats he'd made a thousand times: "Donnie, people who talk end up six feet under. Betrayers are executed. People who tell have accidents." I could still hear him as if it were yesterday.

No, I didn't ever want to tell. I didn't want anyone to know, didn't want to be in this courtroom going through this searing pain of shame and embarrassment. And I was terrified that one day he would carry out his threats. After all, he kept a gun with him all the time.

The secret that I'd kept for a lifetime might have gone with me to the grave, but now I knew he hadn't stopped. He wouldn't stop until someone stopped him. I forced my attention away from the conflicting feelings within to focus on the harsh details of reality. Now there was another four-year-old girl living in terror. Who else could protect little Keely but me? I remembered how I'd felt the thousands of nights when I'd prayed that someone, somehow would protect me. But no one had.

The vision of Keely standing in front of me so paralyzed with fear that she could not speak loomed sharply into focus. She had stood there coughing and choking and stuffing, always stuffing her handkerchief into her tiny mouth.

And just last month she haltingly had choked out what Grandpa had been doing to her.

Part I
Growing Up

As I look at the image in the faded photograph, I can hardly believe the lovely little girl, all blond and sun-kissed, is really me and the handsome man holding me so proudly is my dad. We've been through so much since the photographer captured this tender moment almost half a century ago, yet there we are, having our day in the sun, forever smiling.

This picture of a precious child and her strong young father suggests the idyllic family life in California one envies on snowy winter days back East. It's not hard to fill in the details: endless ocean reaching beyond the horizon, miles of pristine golden sand under an intense blue sky, that clean salt-air smell, gulls circling overhead. Trips to the water's edge to splash in the gentle surf. Sand pails, sea shells, joy, love, laughter.

Yes, from the pictures taken that January day in 1949, I can see how the Landis family might be the envy of everyone. At least until the whole truth of who we were came out.

April 1948
Venice, California

"Wake up, Donna," my own voice comforted me as I came into consciousness. "You're only having that same old dream."

I awoke feeling breathless and out of sorts again. It was the dream I'd had during so many afternoon naps, the one in which the peach blanket on my bunk bed was all messed up and I couldn't stand the rumples down near my feet. In my dream I couldn't get the blanket to be perfectly smooth no matter how hard I tried.

I rolled over on my back to breathe more easily, and soon my thumb and index finger were rubbing the satiny corner of my blanket while I stared at the ceiling. I was vaguely aware of the squeak of the oil pump next door dipping up and down, up and down, pumping oil from under the sand. A slight breeze wafted through, bringing the faint aroma of oil along with sea air.

My mind drifted back to Sunday. It had been an especially nice beach day. Usually the surf rolled right up to the front yard fence, but Sunday the tide was so low that the beach seemed to go on forever, glistening jewel-like against the receding water.

Our whole family had fanned out to see what we could find in the wet sand. Daddy was walking barefoot with my little sister Sandy on his shoulders. I went ahead near Mom, hoping to get beautiful shells.

"Donnie, come over here," she yelled excitedly. I looked up and saw her bending over something in the sand, and for an instant I felt so much love for her. She was slim, girlish and beautiful in her flowered bathing suit, with her long blond hair falling around her face as she examined something in her hand.

I raced over in response to her urgent tone and peered at the strange object.

"What is it?"

Mom held a perfect sand dollar in her palm. The design on the front looked like a beautiful flower. She turned it over.

"What do you see?" Her tone was warm and encouraging. She liked to teach us about our world.

"The purple bottom is all wiggly. Mommy, why is it wiggly?"

"Because it's still alive, Donnie. The ones we usually find are dead. The purple shows us its life."

"Can I touch it?"

"Be very gentle."

The thrill of discovering this wonderful new creature bubbled up in me and I had to run and get Sandy and Dad. He put Sandy down so she could touch it, too.

"Sandy, it's alive," I squealed as the reluctant three- year-old tested it gingerly with one tiny finger.

Daddy led us single file out near the waterline and carefully buried our sand dollar in the sand so it would have a chance to live.

It had really been the best afternoon! Mommy helped us build sandcastles and put baby sand crabs in the courtyard so that the castle would have some people in it, and Daddy skipped stones over the surface of the sea while we watched enthralled. One, two...seven skips. Mom and Sandy and I tried but none of us could get close. Daddy was the champion stone skipper. He was so handsome and muscular, he could do anything. Everyone was always saying he and Mom were a beautiful couple and on this sun-drenched afternoon they were, in every sense of the word. We seemed to be a magic family living in an enchanted circle of love. And still, deep inside, I was holding my breath, hoping it would last.

It didn't seem to matter that we didn't even have a real house and lived in a one-room beach bungalow. But when we got back there that night, it seemed pathetically small and confining, with its green couch in the middle and two sets of bunk beds along the walls. Sandy and I took our bath almost too tired to giggle at our usual game of slippery bumping cars in the tub.

Mom and Dad got through the evening without yelling at each other, but later that night when they thought we were asleep, I heard Dad swearing under his breath at Mom when he pushed his way into the lower bunk with her. Then came the muffled sounds of struggle and surrender that were so familiar, yet so upsetting.

I found myself trying to push the scene from my mind as I lay in my bunk that Tuesday afternoon and became aware that I had been rubbing the satiny edge of my peach blanket back and forth furiously all this time. I didn't know why I should have to sleep in the afternoon like a baby anyway, but our babysitter Mimi made us. She seemed bored taking care of us. I didn't like weekdays at all. I usually felt lonely but there was nothing I could do about it. Dad had to go to work at his auto body shop and Mom had to take her opera lessons.

I should have been in kindergarten, but the class was full by the time Mom took me to register at Nightingale Elementary. I was so disappointed. I was five and longed to go to school; ached to get away from our dingy cottage and make new friends. But I was stuck at home for another year, doomed to taking dumb naps and staring around the room at uneven seams of tape Daddy had used to put up the drywall.

"Aristocrats," my dad had always called us. "Never forget you're an aristocrat, Donna. Your name means 'gracious lady' for a reason. You're going to be somebody some day." His voice still lingers in my ears.

The Landis family was a rare species, real native Californians in a state rapidly becoming populated with outlanders from other states. World Word II had ended and people who had shipped out of California ports to the Pacific or had come to work in its defense plants decided to settle here for good. But my parents were born and raised in Los Angeles, a true son and daughter of the Golden State.

On my father's side, the Landises were pharmacists who had owned the first chain of drug stores in Los Angeles. Family legend has it that they were so rich my great aunt was nicknamed "Hats" at Los Angeles High in the 1890s because she owned more hats, the status symbol of the times, than any other girl in school. My grandfather, Big Ray, still owned a drugstore and went to work every day. In the great Landis tradition, his only child, my father, had been sent to pharmacy college at the University of Southern California.

My mother was Cecelia Burwick, and her father had a lucrative house-painting business. His daughters were the first generation to go to college. Mom was the third girl in the family and was to go to UCLA with the intention of becoming a teacher like her sisters before her.

My mom and dad had that born-for-each-other look and, in fact, had known each other since they were in sixth grade and started dating in high school. It might have been a foregone conclusion that they would marry but not as soon as they did. With the war and the draft looming, my father insisted that they get married right away or he would break up with Mom. They were only 17 at the time, and she wanted that teaching credential, but she didn't want to lose him. Surprisingly her parents went along with it. He seemed to love her so intensely.

Over the years when Dad and I had our special talks, he often told me the story of how much he'd loved my mom – "Crazy in love," was how he put it. He didn't think he could face college without her.

Mom was just 18 when she was married and became my mother the night she turned 19. She had managed to get in a semester at UCLA even though she was pregnant with me and Dad got in a year of pharmacy college. Mom's father died suddenly when I was six months old. Not long afterwards, Dad was drafted in spite of his status as a married student and Mom was left to manage on her own. Two years later, Dad's bleeding ulcers earned him a medical discharge from the Army. The family story is that he just couldn't tolerate the strain of regimentation or loneliness of life away from his family, and apparently he couldn't take more pharmacy college either.

By the time they were 25, my parents' lives seemed to have taken a serious detour. Instead of facing a promising future as the teacher and pharmacist that they had intended to become, they had nothing. Full of fury, my father insisted that my grandmother let him build a tiny prefab house on her lot at the beach. He would become an auto body man and raise his family there. That was that.

It was there at the beach that the lines were drawn that delineated my life; there that my parents loved and raged, that my sister and I left our tiny footprints in the sand every day and watched them wash out to sea. And there that I set out full of excitement for my first day of school – a day that will be etched in my memory forever.

May 1948
Hollywood

"I have the prettiest girls in Hollywood," Dad used to tell us when he drove us to spend the weekend with our grandparents, Maymie and Big Ray. We must have made a charming sight, my movie-star handsome dad at the wheel of our new Ford sedan with his beautiful wife by his side and two wide-eyed little blonds in the back seat.

Sandy and I loved the drive from the beach to town. On a clear day we could see the mountains off in the distance, beyond the enormous flat basin of L.A., with its tall palms reaching towards blue sky. We never got tired of that trip into the sprawling city and the warmth of our grandparents' home. Maymie and Big Ray lived in a fine one-story English Tudor house in the stylish Wilshire District, right across from Farmer's Market.

The house was surrounded by an inviting green lawn and good climbing trees where birds liked to nest. I remember loving all that green so much. And when Maymie opened the oversized oak door of the house, she always greeted us girls with a big smile and hug as she drew us into the wonders of her world, so different from our house at the beach. Shiny oak floors were covered with Persian rugs, and every room was furnished with antiques. China cabinets were everywhere. Maymie was a tireless world traveler who had brought home beautiful antique dolls, fine bone china and other treasures from the corners of the earth. She displayed them in every room of the house except Big Ray's.

My grandfather was 66 years old, 20 years older than his vivacious wife. He was toothless and balding, but his role of family leader guaranteed everyone's tolerance of his eccentricities. He didn't like dentists, or doctors for that matter, and had never learned to drive. He slept in a small room behind the breakfast nook – the room that was meant for a live-in maid. Apparently it had been a long time since he and Maymie had shared a bedroom, and no one thought it was strange at all that he'd made this tiny room his own while Maymie had the biggest bedroom with the most elaborate furniture and best rugs in the house. Her headboard was unforgettable: a sunset depicted in fine inlaid cherry wood.

It was always so much fun to stay with Maymie and Big Ray. Sandy and I got to share a huge bedroom, just the two of us. We loved to snuggle under the blue down comforter in the carved oak bed and listen to the birds chirping outside the windows.

"Wake up, you little sleepy heads. Time to get up," Maymie called in her rich musical voice as she opened the door of our room. The smoky smell of bacon made us want to bounce out of bed.

"Donna, hurry up and you can pick out the dishes for breakfast,"

Maymie knew how I loved to look at her beautiful china. I quickly set the table with plates decorated with bright roses and got out the funny glasses our grandfather had brought home especially for Sandy and me. We had shared conspiratorial giggles when Big Ray whispered how "naughty" those glasses were. There was a girl on the front dressed in a maid's uniform, but from the back her uniform disappeared as we drank our milk, leaving her backside naked.

Then it was time to wake up Big Ray. I knocked softly at his door, "Big Eyes, it's time to eat." Members of our family had many affectionate names for one another.

Big Ray always came out fully dressed, ready for his day. He wore a long-sleeved shirt and dark slacks, with his glasses perched on his prominent nose. He was tall and thin, over 6 foot 2. And I was sure he was the kindest man in the whole world.

"Hi, Princess! How are you this beautiful morning?" He gently picked me up and hugged me to his chest as he seated himself at the table. He always made me feel special and I loved him so much.

"You had a bad night, didn't you?" He looked into my eyes with concern. "You were gnashing your teeth something terrible again. It can't be good for your teeth."

"I don't remember, Big Ray." I was mystified.

Big Ray went on, "I tried to wake you up so that you would stop. Don't you remember? I patted your back for a while until you quieted down."

"Eat up, everyone," Maymie interrupted. "I'm taking the girls to Orbach's today for some new clothes. Their clothes look like they belong to the ragpickers. Then we're going to stop at the Farmer's Market for ice cream!"

"You girls have fun. I'm going to the park to play checkers," Big Ray responded. No one was surprised. That's what he did every weekend.

It didn't take too much encouragement to get Sandy and me ready for a trip to the store. We often went shopping with Maymie and came home with something wonderful. I think she bought us most of our clothes.

Sometimes we went to Big Ray's drugstore with him, and especially loved twirling around on the stools at the soda fountain. Bernie, the teenager who worked behind the counter, made us extra big drinks and we thought she was neat.

On summer evenings when we stayed in town, Sandy and I loved to wait outside for Big Ray to come home from the drugstore on the bus. In the gathering dusk, we played on the steel guard bar that protected the street light in front of the house. It was just the right height for us to somersault over, though it was easier for me than for my little sister. In the glow of the street lamp, I would place my hands on the bar, lift my right leg over it, straddle the bar, then go over. I'd whirl over and over on the bar as fast as I could until I could see Big Ray's tall form approaching in the pale light of streetlights across the street.

We squealed and jumped up and down with excitement as he got closer, but obediently waited on our side of the street. Finally he would scoop us up in his arms and carry us both inside.

"Whoa, there! Slow down, girls."

We could hardly wait for him to sit down and show us the treat he'd brought. We'd race to get on his lap.

"Donna, you climb up on this knee, Sandy, you climb up over here. Hold this bag. I've got a surprise for my girls. No peeking!"

Big Ray was as delighted with our little treats as we were, and we loved his big toothless grin as he watched us joyfully dig inside the bag for candy or toys.

After a light dinner, which always included easy-to-chew milk toast, he loved to tell us bedtime stories. We'd climb on his lap once again and the stories would go on until Maymie insisted that we get ready for bed.

His stories were fabulous. We heard tales of horse-and-buggy days in Los Angeles; how he outsmarted teachers at Los Angeles High in 1901, how he handled robbers in a holdup at his drug store.

Though he passed away years ago, I can still hear Big Ray's voice telling the stories that let us know we had a real place in this city. I felt anchored and at home on visits to my grandparents' house. I don't know who I would have grown up to be if it hadn't been for their love and influence. To this day collecting antiques and hand-painted china are important activities that enrich my life. I know I got my love of beautiful things from Maymie.

But there was something that didn't make sense about our living on the edge of poverty at the beach while my grandparents had so much. In my child's mind I couldn't formulate the questions and would probably have been afraid to ask them anyway. I always felt threatened by the ferocity of rage my father could summon. He was totally charming, yet capable of flying off the handle unexpectedly at all of us – his wife, his children, his parents.

Years later, when the whole story came to light, I knew I could not have handled the truth until I was much older and wiser and had a solid support system. I was already dealing with as much as I could.

January 1949
First Grade
Venice Beach

Early in the morning at the body shop, I was nervous while my parents were working. I kept Sandy out of their way, but my thoughts were on school. Today was the first day of first grade. It was finally here! I was careful not to let the dust and masking tape on the floor stick to my new maroon oxfords. I wanted them to still look new by the time I got to school. It was bad enough having to get Daddy to show me which one fit my right foot...when would I get them straight?

As the time to leave for school drew near, I overheard my parents arguing over who was going to take me. Mom insisted that she would, but Dad overruled her.

"Goddamit, Cecelia, you haven't even finished sanding the right fender yet. I've got to spray this thing this afternoon; I can't do everything around here myself, for God's sake! I'll take Donnie while you finish up. Make sure those windows are properly masked too."

I climbed up into the front seat of our car, a brand-new light green Ford, and said goodbye to Mommy. As she kissed my cheek, she seemed kind of sad. I knew she wished she could take me.

I waved a last goodbye. I felt so special. A big girl at last! As we drove away from the shop, I thought about making new friends, about all the fun I would have with the kids at recess. I always watched them hitting a big red ball against the schoolyard fence.

Suddenly I looked up. This was not the way to school. This was the way back to our house. I could see the small stucco and frame cottages that made up the beach-front housing area. It was mostly empty lots and oil wells, with an occasional estate owned by a Hollywood mogul oddly juxtaposed against the ugly wells.

I could see dozens of wells set between little beach bungalows. Some of the wells had tall derricks and others were squat. All had rusty corrugated fencing surrounding their machinery.

Venice was desolate on this bleak January day. Sparsely populated at best on the weekends of summer, now in winter there was no one around except an occasional workman, dressed in oil-stained coveralls and a metal construction hat.

"Daddy, I have to get to school, why are we going to our house?" I asked. I was alarmed.

"There's plenty of time. I forgot something."

I was not reassured. When we got to the house, I pressed back against the seat, not wanting to get out of the car.

"Come on, Donnie!" urged Dad in silky tone.

"Daddy, I have to get to school," I pleaded.

"There's plenty of time."

It was his "no-nonsense" voice. I knew better than to argue with *that* voice. Reluctantly I climbed out of the car as Daddy unlocked the door to the house. Once inside, he pulled me into a hug. "I love you more than anything, my little bugger," he whispered into my ear. Perhaps he sensed my frustration, for he immediately started to tickle my tummy. I always liked to play tickle. Giggling, and breathless from squirming around, I soon forgot the time. I loved my Daddy's attention.

"Donnie, betcha can't hide from me," he laughed.

"Betcha I can!" I taunted between giggles. "Close your eyes, Daddy. No! You have to cover them with your hands!" I reached for his hands and placed them over his eyes. "Now count to ten real slow!"

Hide and seek was our favorite game and I was good at it. I sneaked past him with light footsteps, and hid under the dinette table. The long oilcloth came down over my face. I held my breath. Dad pretended he couldn't find me and looked in all corners.

Too soon, he discovered my hiding place. "Got you, you little bugger."

I was giggling so hard I could not stop. It was so funny. Daddy was tickling me and laughing. Suddenly he stopped laughing and his mood seemed to change. He became serious and agitated. I noticed a faint line of perspiration across his brow and his hands were shaking. What was going on? I was afraid.

He got weird, and started touching me in a strange way. It was not tickles now. It was under my panties.

"Hey, no!" I yelled. My laughter died in my throat. "Hey, no...," I cried out. "What're you doing?" I pulled my legs together and tried to get up from where he'd pinned me down in our tickling match.

"Daddy, no! Stop touching me!" I protested, but my six-year-old cries did no good. This was a hulk of a man who lifted weights before dinner. This was a man who flexed his muscles as he ripped the six-inch phone book down the middle. This was a man who called himself a 180-pound gorilla. I was no match for Dad.

I grew still but it was not his strength that quieted me. It was a ferocity I sensed behind his eyes. He ignored me, said nothing and began to rub me under my panties while he did something funny to himself with his other hand. In spite of my pleas, he would not stop. It was exactly as if he had not heard me at all.

He seemed to be staring off into the distance when I briefly caught his eye. He stood up, zipped his pants and said in a deadly serious tone, "Donnie, you're not to tell anyone about this. Not your mother or Maymie or Big Ray, not Sandy or your Aunt Margie. No one! You are to tell no one!"

His words were clear, and some deep, unspoken force communicated with intensity that words never could. I was not to tell. His icy blue eyes threatening me, warning me, demanding that I never tell, put such a spell on me that I froze to the borders of my being.

I would not tell, but the fear I felt was like a big lump in my throat. Somewhere near my heart, I felt an ugly hole of shame opening. I would never tell. But I would always feel the searing edges of that hollow opening deep within.

Finally Daddy took me to school. I was upset and I was late. But mostly I was terrified. School was never as wonderful as I had dreamed it would be. It was dark somehow when I had yearned for light. I know that I never really fit in. I felt so different. I might as well have had a mark across my forehead.

Eventually I was able to make one friend. Geraldine Renee. We enjoyed orange juice and graham crackers at recess and got especially good at twirling around in circles.

The spinning was so neat! I had three dresses, but my favorite was a soft green one with a full skirt and sash that Aunt Margie, my mother's sister, had bought for me. I washed it out at night so that it was ready again for twirling. When we twirled, my skirt would spread out in a floating arc. I loved to twirl. It helped me forget.

In the evenings before I went to bed, I pulled the dinette chair up the kitchen sink and washed out my green dress and ankle socks. I noticed that the other girls had clean dresses and bright white socks, and I tried hard to be like them. I only had one pair of socks so I washed them carefully and hung them to dry on the back of the chair near the portable floor heater. I even learned to iron my dress. On special days, I pinned my hair into what I hoped would be curls so that I would be pretty for twirling. Mommy praised me for all this activity and said I was a big girl, but she never helped.

Even with Geraldine, the graham crackers and twirling, first grade had many dark days. I was not sure why.

The worst day was May Day when the teacher told all of us to form a big circle on the playground to learn the May Day dance. I felt embarrassed and ugly when the children on either side of me recoiled when they saw my warts. Neither child would take my hand. "She's got cooties! She's got cooties," they jeered.

The teacher ordered them to hold hands with me, but it really didn't make me feel better.

To this day, May Day brings that old memory back to me.

March 1950
Venice Beach

"For chrissake, Cecelia, the girls have green teeth." Dad's voice rose to a full-decibel shout. "Their necks are dirty. Why the hell can't you even keep them clean?"

"Why can't you keep Bernie out of our house?" Mom yelled back.

"At least she wouldn't dress the girls in blue jeans," Dad shot back. "You keep my girls out of those goddam things! They're going to grow up to be ladies. And ladies do not wear jeans."

My mother seemed to get smaller when Dad yelled at her. My parents had always argued about everything – especially about us kids. But when Bernie came to live in our driveway, their arguments became especially vicious. I wasn't sure exactly why, because Bernie seemed like a nice enough girl, but that seemed to be a turning point for our family. Mom had always been a little distant, but she seemed to lose her commitment to family life after that and never seemed sharply focused on us again. She retreated further into her world of singing lessons and college classes.

Dad had dragged a battered old wooden house trailer into our driveway and moved Bernie into it. She was 17, overweight and had mouse-colored braids pinned on the top of her head. She wore little makeup and never looked nearly as beautiful as my glamorous mother. Bernie had worked at Big Ray's soda fountain, which my parents were now running, and Dad decided that she would make a good babysitter. At least that's what he told us. I was just seven, Sandy was five, and we still needed someone to take care of us.

Bernie and Mom sat together sometimes and shared Ovaltine at our little dinette table. Usually they commiserated with each other about my Dad. Even so, Mom was always complaining to Dad about Bernie's coming into our house at all hours to use the bathroom. It was hard to understand the world of grown-ups. I found the best way to handle it was to be quiet and do what I was told.

I got along fine with Bernie. She was much better than any of our other babysitters, and I grew quite comfortable with her. She seemed to like me, too, and as time went on, we came to love each other.

Dad took care of Sandy and me quite often and liked to take us on excursions to the fun places on the beach. We always looked forward to going to the fun zone at Venice Pier and to the amusement center at Ocean Park where we played in the rolling barrels and laughed ourselves sick in front of the curvy mirrors. Sandy and I liked to run back and forth, watching ourselves turn from short and fat to tall and thin and back again. Dad seemed to enjoy it as much as we did, and we all laughed when the mechanical fat lady, Laughing Sal, cackled.

One weekend Daddy packed me into our car and we drove all the way to Big Bear Lake, just the two of us. We drove for miles across the Los Angeles basin, then headed out east of the city toward Palm Springs, through country that looked more and more like desert with every passing mile.

On the way he talked about Bernie and Mom, and I listened hard.

"Donnie, you understand why I have Bernie, don't you? Your mother is frigid."

I didn't have any idea what that meant, but I nodded sagely. I was used to my parents talking to me as if I understood what they meant.

Dad reached over and patted my hand. "That's my girl, Donnie. You know, Bernie is lucky to have me. I could have anyone I want, but I want to stay with your mother for the sake of you girls."

I was glad to hear they were going to stay together, and I nodded again, this time with more enthusiasm.

"I could have married really old money. Mary Blank, the candy heiress, man did she want me! She's a fine lady. A real aristocrat," he lectured on, caught up in his reverie. His eyes narrowed and his tone changed as he continued, "Bernie is lower class. I'm not hurting her. She doesn't have such good chances. She'll let me stay with your mother."

At the base of the San Bernardino Mountains we found the steep, winding road up to Big Bear, and Dad grew quiet as he negotiated the switchback curves. The air got cooler as we drew closer to the top and pine forests edged the road. At the top of the mountain, we saw huge granite boulders strewn along the shore of the lake as if a crazy giant had hurled them from the sky.

We stopped at a country store that looked like something out of a Wild West movie. A faded wooden sign across the tattered screen door announced, "Coca-Cola." Inside it was dimly lit, but my eyes fell on a jar of fresh oatmeal cookies sitting on the counter. They looked delicious!

Dad noticed my interest right away. "Honey, do you want one of those big ol' cookies?"

"May I? I love them."

Dad nodded to the storekeeper and she asked me with a smile, "Which one would you like?"

My eyes were just at the level of the cookie jar and I surveyed them seriously.

"The one right there with the most raisins, please." I pointed out the biggest cookie in the jar.

Dad and the storekeeper laughed and seemed to be enjoying this as much as I was.

"You sure have a polite little girl, Mister," she commented.

Dad paid for the cookie and it was fresh and fragrant. It turned out to be the best thing about that trip. I ate it slowly, savoring its crunchy goodness for as long as I could. I had an idea of what was coming.

We checked into a rustic log cabin that had just one creaky bed, and I tried to think about that wonderful cookie when Dad did things to me in the dark.

When I resisted, he caught my small wrist and twisted my arm hard enough to break the elbow, easily pinning me down. But I believed him when he told me I was his special girl and he loved me more than anything. He hurt me, but said over and over that all this special attention was proof that he loved me. I pushed my scared feelings away, trying very hard not to have them, and remembered that cookie again.

I didn't have to be warned anymore. I would never tell on Daddy. Somewhere in the back of my mind I knew if I told Mommy, she would go crazy and I would lose her forever. That idea scared me even more than the awful things Daddy was doing to me.

We had many weekend trips after that, just the two of us, but the trip to Big Bear is the one I remember the most clearly.

Years later, when I was in my 40s, my husband and I took our three children up there on a family ski trip, and we passed that same log cabin, the strewn boulders. A flash of that trip with Dad crowded my consciousness and that awful night came back, leaving me panicked, breathless, smelling that oatmeal cookie again as if it were only yesterday. I gulped air to maintain equilibrium. My husband and children must not know anything was wrong. No, I would not tell. I would never tell. I clung to the armrest on the passenger door. I had to steady myself.

Spring 1950
Venice Beach

"Mommy, look what I got for you." My heart was full as I skipped in the door with a big red rose wrapped in newspaper. Our neighbor down the beach had noticed me admiring her rose bushes and had cut the most beautiful flower for me to give to my mother. I was so proud. I just knew it would make her smile.

But no one was home at our house. The sound of angry voices coming from Bernie's trailer broke into my happy fantasy.

"Who knocked you up, you goddam whore?" Dad's voice grew louder and louder. "I know you've been out screwing around every time I turn my back," he yelled.

I ran to the trailer in time to see Bernie's face contort with anguish. "No! No! I didn't. No one," was all she could manage between sobs.

"Don't lie, you stupid bitch. It was the lifeguard. I know you, always hanging around those muscleheads." He sounded as if he were about to take a swing at her.

"Stop yelling! Do you want the whole world to know?" Mom chimed in.

"You stay out of this, Cecelia. It's between Bernie and me. She's gotta take a lie detector test, goddam it. I know she's been out screwing around."

He turned his fury back to Bernie and she cowered under its force. "You go take a lie detector test or you're never going to see me again. I'll throw you right out on the street. Let your lifeguard take care of you."

If they had asked me, I would have told them that Bernie only talked about the undertow with Kip, the lifeguard who manned the tower near our house. I knew. I had been with her. But no one asked me. They raged on, the three of them, until Mom stormed out of Bernie's trailer.

"I don't know why I get into these things," she muttered to no one in particular. "It really doesn't matter to me."

I didn't know what that meant, but must have been something terrible that happened to poor Bernie. Mom seemed awfully unhappy about it. I put the rose in a glassful of water for her and she hugged me, but she didn't really smile.

Later that night Mom brought up Bernie again when she thought we were asleep.

"Who's going to support your bastard?" she whispered furiously to Dad. "It's bad enough you have to park your girlfriend in the driveway and get her pregnant, now you're going to have to support another child. And with what?"

Dad didn't care whether we were awake or asleep. "I told you, it wasn't me. Bernie's been screwing around," he shouted. "Besides, my family's rich. They'll always come through with the money."

"I haven't seen much around here for your real family, much less Bernie's baby."

Dad was quiet for a minute.

Mom went on, "She can't keep that baby around here, Ray. She just can't. Everyone will know you're screwing her."

"Get off my back, Cecelia. I'll do whatever I goddam want with Bernie, and you can't stop me. Now shut the fuck up."

I couldn't tell whether Mom was crying or not. Mostly when Dad yelled at her, she just looked sad, so very sad. I wished with all my heart that the rose had made her smile.

"Listen, Sandy! I can hear a baby cry." I shook my little sister's shoulder with excitement. "Can you hear it?"

Sandy looked puzzled, and her eyes rolled upward as she listened intently.

"There it is again. You can hear it, Sandy. Just listen harder."

Between the sounds of cars whizzing by on Washington Boulevard, I was sure I could hear the faint cry of a baby.

Sandy and I stood outside the hospital, pressed against the windows, trying to stay cool under the overhanging roof. The heat was incredible for a June day. We weren't allowed to go into the hospital when Mom and Dad went to see Bernie, so we stood outside the window, cupped our hands against the dusty screen and tried to peer in. I could barely make out shapes in the shadows, but as my eyes became accustomed to the gloom, I was pretty sure I saw four women lying in beds along the walls. One of them waved to me so I guessed that must be Bernie. Was that her baby I could hear?

Sandy and I liked to play dolls, but we had never had a real baby to play with. I was so excited I couldn't stand still. "A real baby, Sandy. We have a real baby!"

When we got home I got out my Betsy Wetsy doll, gave her a bottle and changed her diaper when she wet on cue. I had to practice as hard as I could for when Bernie's baby came home. I had never held a real baby and could only imagine how it would feel.

A few days later Mom and Dad went back to the hospital to pick up Bernie and her new baby. But they didn't come home to our house. Dad had found a new apartment for Bernie in a garage facing an alley off a back street. When we went in, it seemed really tiny, and I noticed right away it didn't have a bathroom. There was a white porcelain pan behind a curtain for Bernie to go to the bathroom in. I thought that was odd. There was no sink and the water came from a hose in the backyard.

Bernie sat down with the baby, and I got to look at her. She had brown hair like Bernie's, a pink wrinkled face and the tiniest little hands I'd ever seen.

"What's her name, Bernie?" I whispered.

"Cee Cee. That's short for Cecelia," Bernie replied, smiling down at her infant daughter with great tenderness.

I had to think about that for a minute. I wondered why Bernie's baby was named after my mom, but decided not to ask questions. I wasn't sure how relationships worked, but in some deep way I knew that Cee Cee and I were family.

Cee Cee started to cry. So much noise from such a little girl! Mom took her from Bernie and rocked her gently, but Cee Cee kept right on crying.

Mom handed her back to Bernie who tried to soothe her tears.

"Come on, Donnie," Mom said, taking my hand and leading me outside. "Let's go to the store and buy Cee Cee some blankets and clothes. It doesn't look like there's anything here for that poor little baby at all."

Mom was gentle and loving with Cee Cee, but her voice was always filled with anger when she spoke to my father. The whole feeling in our home changed and there was a noticeable lack of warmth between Mom and Dad. Gone were the long sunny days when the four of us skipped stones on the beach.

Mom spent less and less time with us. She had a job now on the playground and still kept up with her opera classes. Some nights she didn't get in until very late. Once we overhead her telling Dad all about her new boyfriend, and he did not seem to mind. They confided secrets in the dark sometimes, like old friends, in contrast to their fierce arguments by day. I felt uneasy, unsure about what was happening to our family, but I knew better than to ask.

Not long after Cee Cee was born, Dad took me aside and warned me in those now familiar grave tones, "Donnie, if anyone asks you about this new baby, you are to tell them her name is Cee Cee Davis, and her father was killed in a taxi cab crash in Chicago."

It was a hard speech to remember but I tried to keep all the "C" words together as we had been taught in school – cab, crash, Chicago. I could do it.

"You'd better remember, Donnie."

I nodded, "Okay."

"I'm not kidding Donnie. It's a secret who her real father is. You are to tell the truth to no one."

I wasn't sure about her real father, but I understood about not telling the truth. He could count on me. I wasn't going to tell. I always behaved like a good little girl – a good little girl who grew warts on her hands, ground her teeth at night and occasionally wet the bed.

I ground my teeth and wet my bed alone, so no one knew, but the warts were different. They made my hands so ugly, and it was hard to keep them hidden. I wondered where those warts came from. I didn't have them when I was younger, before first grade, before Daddy started to take me to school in the mornings.

February 1951
Venice Beach

"Let us in! Please let us in. We'll be good."

Sandy and I were shivering and crying but the door wouldn't open. We were locked out again on the pitch black beach with the angry surf pounding a few yards away and nothing but spooky oil wells to keep us company. They looked like a herd of metal dinosaurs dipping up and down in the eerie light of the new moon, creaking and moaning, "kuh plump, kuh plump," as they brought up thick, foul-smelling oil.

My little sister and I were no strangers to the night. We were often locked out as punishment for making noise or playing too spiritedly. It was always scary out there with the night sounds.

It was also frightening to be left in charge of Sandy and Cee Cee at Bernie's new apartment, but I was often the babysitter when my dad took Bernie out. She had moved to a new place when Cee Cee was seven months old. I loved it during the day: it had a stove, a little patio and even a real bathroom. There were about 12 children to play with in the family next door and we had all kinds of fun. They were poor, but their house echoed with laughter and smelled of homemade bread. After dark, though, if I got frightened, it would never occur to me to knock on their door and ask for help.

I worried about Cee Cee's wobbly little head and tried hard to handle her gently. She was a darling baby and I loved to hug her and play with her, but I was concerned about hurting her and about making her bottle right. Turning the gas on seemed dangerous if I didn't strike the match, I would have blown us up. And I didn't want to overheat the milk and scald her mouth.

Sandy would usually come with me when I took care of Cee Cee. If Bernie and Dad stayed out late, we'd be afraid of every sound outside. After I'd lay Cee Cee in her crib, I'd shush Sandy and tiptoe to the back door to make sure it was bolted. Eventually Sandy and I would fall asleep clinging to each other in a big chair, listening hard for strange noises over the sound of the oil wells and the wind rustling through the palm trees.

We stayed at Bernie's apartment a lot while my mother was busy, and she was busy almost every day with her job and with practice for the opera. On Saturdays when she was home, she'd lie on the floor with our huge dictionary perched on her diaphragm while she vocalized.

"May, me, mou, mu-u-u-u-u," Mom sang out, holding her notes as long as possible to strengthen her abdominal muscles.

"May, me, mou, mu," Sandy and I echoed as we ran though the house giggling.

"Enough noise," Dad shouted. "You girls get the hell out of here and go play! Don't bother your mother."

We were used to not bothering Mom, so we went outside to the driveway where we found the beautiful old 1936 Chevrolet they were restoring. Mom had meticulously painted it by hand. It had four doors that opened from the center post, and was the perfect place to play stagecoach.

Sandy and I hid from Indian attacks in the back seat. As imaginary desperados and Indians stalked us from behind the oil well next door, we grew excited.

"They're coming. Look out!" I screamed.

"Get down!" squealed Sandy, slamming the door to keep the bad guys out.

As the game heated up, we slammed the doors over and over, and by the end of the day, each of us had managed to break our index finger.

Mom was furious. She could not believe that we would be so stupid. My sister and I chalked it all up to a rough day on the range, but Mom shook her head at us as she tried to fix our broken fingers. Our oddly curved fingers would attest to that Indian attack for the rest of our years.

Decades later Sandy demanded that Mom explain why she let us play in that dangerous way and why our fingers were not set by a doctor. I never gave it a second thought. Perhaps I did not expect much from anyone. I was usually careful to be a good girl but sometimes Sandy and I played dangerous games, especially after she started afternoon kindergarten at Nightingale and we spent our after-school hours together. I'm not sure why I needed to be daring. Perhaps it was because I had so little control over my own body that I felt pushing my limits gave me a sense of being in charge of my life.

During the years that Mom was a playground leader, Sandy and I used to walk up to Venice Beach where she worked after school. On the way we'd skip along Windward Avenue on the covered sidewalks of the quietly decaying buildings with their once majestic colonnades, now home to an odd collection of winos, bums and other bizarre characters.

Everyone along the boardwalk knew us, two little towheaded girls holding hands, making their way to the playground where their mother worked, where it was safe. We never talked to strangers even though they talked to us. We had been warned time and time again about bad men who would lure little girls into cars with candy, and we took those warnings very seriously. I did not want to get yelled at or get locked out in the night, and I certainly did not want anything bad to happen to little Sandy.

Mom would wait for us at the entrance to the playground, which was just in front of the rotting old pier at Venice Beach, but after that, she'd have to ignore us, not wanting her supervisor to get angry at her for having her children hanging around. We pretended we were not her children. We practiced being invisible.

Once I did have an important question. I sneaked over to the office and stood staring at the floor until Mom wasn't busy. The red cement of the game area was covered with a fine white layer of sand. I tried to be quiet, but I couldn't wait any longer.

"Mommy, what religion am I? That big girl over on the swings wants to know."

"You're Protestant, Donnie," she answered matter of factly.

It didn't mean anything to me, but at least I had a category to fit into.

One day Sandy and I sneaked off the fenced-in play yard with Elsa, an 11-year-old who often came to the playground with her little dog, a small brown dachshund named Hans. We darted past "No Trespassing" signs and the boarded-up entrance to the pier, which had long since been considered too dangerous for visitors. Elsa picked up her dog and ran out to the pier, along the narrow walkway between the old arcade building and the sheer drop to the pounding surf below.

"Come on Donna. It's fun!" she dared.

I was frightened. "It's too high! It's scary," I yelled across the distance to her. I noticed poor little Hans was shaking in her arms.

"Chicken, chicken," she taunted.

Sandy was silently standing next to me. I looked at the surf rising and falling beneath me. I could see white sea foam between the rough boards of the rickety pier, which shook under the pounding of the waves.

"There's no rail. What if I fall?" I yelled into the winter afternoon.

"Just be careful, you yellow chicken."

With that I took a deep breath and stepped out onto the splintery foot-wide ledge. Gingerly, I placed one foot in front of the other, taking tiny steps, inching my way along the length of the building. It seemed to take an eternity. I looked up at Elsa once, but it was a mistake. She looked mean; as if she hoped I would fall into the ocean and get swept away. My heart began to pound even harder but I couldn't stop now. I speeded up, taking the last few steps quickly. I made it!

I looked back at my little sister, and shouted, "Don't try it, Sandy! Don't come out here,"

I don't know whether she could hear me over the sound of the wind and surf, but from the terrified look on her face, I knew she wouldn't try.

Elsa's little dachshund was shivering, seeming to understand that one false step and we could be killed. Without saying anything to Elsa I gathered my courage and started back. With the wind gusting around me, I put one foot in front of the other very carefully and, step by step, made my way back toward safety.

At last I was at my sister's side. We were both petrified. We both looked back at the big girl clutching her little dog, trying to make her way to safety, too, no longer taunting, but as terrified as we were. Finally they arrived at the safe end of the pier, and we all raced back to the security of the playground, never to venture up there again. We never played with Elsa again, nor did we ever tell a soul what we had done.

For months afterward, I would sit on the swing and stare at that narrow little catwalk. The next year the city tore down that dangerous pier, but I remembered it always and that death-defying walk. I wondered whatever made me take such a big chance.

Summer 1952
Culver City, California

"Come on, Donnie. I want to show you our new house." Dad was beaming. "You'll really like it, honey. It's a beauty. And it's much sunnier than at the beach."

We climbed into the car and shivered as we drove inland through the chill fog that hugs the coast in June. After a few miles, we broke through into the fading sunshine of late afternoon as we reached the little wood-fronted stucco house in Culver City.

I was so excited; I could hardly wait to see it. I brought my new plastic vanity set with me, even though our furniture would not be delivered until the next day. I had bought the little blue comb, brush and mirror with my own money so that I would have something special for my new bedroom.

I skipped up the sidewalk across the tiny green lawn and jumped up and down as Dad unlocked the door. I started to run through the house but he would not let me.

"In a minute you can see it all," he said in that familiar threatening voice.

"Daddy, I want to see everything." I was miserable, knowing what was coming.

"Please, Daddy," I begged.

But he ignored my pleas and led me into the bedroom he would share with Mommy. He made me kneel and bend forwards on my hands and knees, with my head inside the closet.

"Hold still," he demanded.

I was used to hearing "hold still.' He always said that to me, since the first day of school when we played hide and seek.

I clutched my hair brush in my hand while he touched me with his fingers under my panties. I prayed it would be over soon. I had trained myself to separate away from myself and concentrate on something else while Daddy did what he always did to himself with his other hand. This time I kept my mind focused on the new house.

Later Daddy let me see all the rooms.

Even though my excitement was diminished by the holding-still episode, I still felt amazed when I walked through the house. It was so much like other children's homes. In the dusky light I could see a real bathroom, real closets and a private room just for Sandy and me.

I was nine years old, and for the first time it looked as if I might have a normal life – at least a life that looked normal. Underneath it all, I felt anything but normal. But I had become good at pretending. I would act as if I did not feel dirty; pretend I did not feel as if I had a mark on my forehead. Pretense was my first line of defense. I could not think of anything else to do.

September 1952
Culver City, California

Now that I was nine, I was excited about starting fourth grade. I was surprised to see that I had a male teacher, Mr. Good. I wasn't too sure what to expect from him and started out the year sitting at the back of the room, staring at the old inkwell hole. But Mr. Good lived up to his name, and soon I began to feel comfortable.

When we shared about our summer vacations, some of the children talked about trips they had taken. I didn't want to tell about any of the day trips Dad had made me take with him, but told about moving from the beach to our new house in Culver City.

When a redhead named Leanne got up and told about sailing on the Sea Gypsy, her parents' new 32-foot sailboat, I thought she was the most beautiful girl I had ever seen. She had freckles all over and a long ponytail with three ringlets in it. I wished I could be like her: beautiful, freckled, redheaded, sweet and self-assured. More than anything, I wished she would be my friend.

Before long, we did become friends. Leanne lived right across the street from our school and invited me over all the time after class. I'll never forget the first time I walked into her house. It was clean like my grandparents' house and smelled of furniture polish. Her mother was always happy to see us. She would smile, laugh with us and interrupt her housework to get us cookies and milk. So this was how mothers behaved!

I took mental notes all the time at Leanne's house. There were stacks of clean, neatly folded clothes at the foot of Leanne's bed, shiny kitchen cabinets, no dust and toys. Everything was neatly stowed away. When Leanne and her mom took me shopping with them at a department store, I was really impressed. I had been going by myself on the bus to W.T. Grant's dime store when I needed something new to wear.

Having Leanne for a friend was the happiest experience of my childhood. I loved her and felt safe and secure at her house. I was there almost every day, and we had great fun playing with her brother's baseball cards, playing jacks or just giggling like crazy about funny things that happened at school. All the other kids thought we were hilarious. We were always laughing until our sides hurt.

That was the year my warts disappeared. I'm not sure I understood what it meant when I read that warts might be psychosomatic, but when my friendship with Leanne brought such happiness into my life, the warts went away.

I had to invite Leanne to visit my home eventually, but I put it off as long as I could. The day before she came, I got busy, raking up leaves in the backyard, sweeping dust and hundreds of candy wrappers from under the twin beds in the room I shared with Sandy. What a mess! Before school I was up early making all the beds and dusting. I ran a load of laundry, folded some of my clothes and stacked them on the end of my bed. I wanted Leanne to think that my mom took care of me the way hers did.

I had learned so much about how normal households worked at Leanne's home, it made it easier to pretend our family was like hers. In fact, it made it imperative. I even wondered out loud what was in my brown paper lunch bag with the rest of the kids in the school lunchroom. Of course, I always knew I had a baloney sandwich and an apple. I made my own lunch every morning and didn't really mind. It just took a minute. But I was envious of the other kids who had someone make their lunches for them. And their breakfasts.

I made many friends that wonderful year in fourth grade, and before long the other girls invited me to join their Brownie troop. It was exciting to think about having a cute little Brownie outfit and going to meetings, and I begged my mother to call the troop leader right away.

When the Brownie leader explained that each girl had to host one meeting and that her mother had to be there for it, my mother looked crestfallen. She still had her job at the park and could not be home to conduct a Brownie meeting. In those "Leave It To Beaver" days of the 1950s, working mothers were rare and looked down on, and their children were often excluded.

"Donnie, sweetheart, I'm so sorry."

"I know Mom. It's okay." It was hard, but I knew Mom felt as bad as I did about it, and I tried to be brave.

"Honey," she continued, "you've talked about nothing but Brownies for weeks now, but I'll make it up to you. We'll do something fun. While I teach crafts next summer, you can join the class. The ladies will love you! We'll make those fiber flowers you like so much. Your very own flowers for your room. You'll like that, won't you, honey?"

I didn't want Mom to feel more sorry for me. She could not help it if she had to work to help support our family.

"Don't worry so much about the Brownies, Mom. The girls are still my friends. I see them every day at school. Leanne still has lots of time to play."

I understood why I could not be a Brownie. I had always understood these things and pretended that I felt okay. I knew I wasn't like the other kids, but I wasn't always so sure why. Even though I was a little confused, I never complained, not even on Thursday, Brownie day, when the other girls wore their uniforms to school and went to their meeting without me. I wanted so much to be a part of that group. Especially when the Brownies had their monthly pajama party at one of the girl's houses. I'd hear in vivid detail how the party had gone and all about their nutty tricks. I acted enthusiastic and laughed at their antics, but deep inside, where the truth hid, I was in terrible pain.

Summer 1953
Culver City

We were glad when summer arrived, and we spilled out of class right into vacation time with its promise of long afternoons at the beach. But that summer between the fourth and fifth grade something happened that sent shock waves through my soul and dimmed the luster of my life.

It started with a fishing trip, an overnight with Dad, up the coast north of Malibu to Sycamore Cove where there was a nice fishing pier.

It began well enough. I was getting good at fishing and caught five fish on one multiple hook at the same time. Five Lucky Joes at once made me feel really proud, and Dad was shouting in excitement so all the other fishermen on the pier could hear. I think I was the only girl there, and I had proved my excellence as a fisherman. I even caught a shark, which was quite a lot for a nine-year-old to land.

Later we had a campfire and ate hot dogs. We always threw the fish back. The Pacific was beautiful that night and stars were visible overhead, even before the sun sank into the lavender waves. As we watched the sky grow dark Dad moved closer and took my face in his hands. Looking into my eyes he smiled softly.

"You're my special girl, Donnie," he whispered, nuzzling me with his face. "I love you more than anything."

I knew what was coming. He was going to have me bend over and hold still for him. I glanced up and down the beach to be sure no one could see us. I didn't want anyone to know how he touched me.

But I was wrong. That isn't what he wanted at all.

Tonight he seemed stronger than ever before as he hugged me to him. He was in his bathing suit, and I could smell the aroma of sweat in the hair of his chest.

Later that night, after I went to sleep in the front bunk, Daddy woke me up. He was naked, which I was used to, but this time he was different. He pushed up my nightie, lay down beside me and began to touch me. I tried not to breathe, tried to fake sleep, but he did not stop for a long time. Then he rolled over on to me, his big naked body right on top of my little one. I felt panicked as he began to breathe faster but still did not call out. What he did to me hurt terribly between my legs. It seemed to go on forever, but at last he was through.

"You're a real woman now, Donnie," he sighed.

But I wasn't. Not at all. I was a frightened nine-year-old who had just been raped by her own father, too terrified to cry out for help. If I had, he would have been furious, would have bent my wrists back until my elbows cracked, shouted, glared at me until ice formed on my soul, left me out all night on the beach and never let me back into the house. If I had tried to defend myself, no punishment would have been too terrible. And it wouldn't have done any good. There was no one there to help me.

I lay there in pain and terror afterwards. My father went back to sleep in his bunk as if nothing had happened. I was so sore I had trouble walking for several days. Was this what it meant to be a real woman?

I wondered about that summer long. While Leanne and my other classmates were chattering about leaving Brownies behind and becoming Girl Scouts, it was hard for me to be with them. My mind seemed stuck in the pain and humiliation of becoming a real woman.

Daddy was after me a lot that summer. He never let me forget.

When September came and it was time to go back to school, I didn't want to go. I didn't want to face all the other children, didn't want them to see me, to look into my face. I was sure that someone would look into my eyes and discover that I was a real woman now. I thought I would die if anyone found out.

September 1953
Culver City

"Don't fuck with me, Donnie," Dad shouted, his face livid with rage. "Get back to work on that car."

"I don't want to," I shouted back. "Working on cars is for boys."

"Don't you dare defy me, goddamit. You're not going to be some bag of fluff, some helpless broad who doesn't know a carburetor from a commode."

As usual, Dad won the argument, and I went back under the hood.

Dad had bought me an old Hudson which needed a new engine. He decided that not only was it time for me to be a real woman, it was also time for me to learn how to rebuild a car. If my friends in fifth grade ever wondered about my family being weird before, this proved it. Whoever heard of buying a girl an old jalopy for her tenth birthday anyway?

The plan was for me to take the engine apart after school and on weekends, and I proceeded to do it through most of the fifth grade. Dad was adamant that I should understand the principles of internal combustion and be able to fix an engine. I hated working on that car. I wanted to ride bikes or talk about lipstick, Kotex or bras to Leanne on the phone, or read Nancy Drew mysteries. But I was afraid to take a stand against my dad's wishes, so I worked on the Hudson.

I missed more school than any other student in fifth grade and didn't care. Leanne was in a different class that semester, so I couldn't see her during the day anyway. And surprisingly, my parents said it was my decision whether I went to school or not.

My new teacher, Mrs. Ferguson, ridiculed me so mercilessly for poor attendance that I preferred to stay home. Besides, it was easier to avoid the other kids than defend myself against them when they teased me about my old car.

Besides the Hudson, I had a new pink sewing machine Dad bought for me at the pawn shop and I liked to sew myself skirts and dresses. I made some for Cee Cee, too, because Bernie didn't know how and the poor little three-year-old was running around in tatters. Mom gave me regular sewing lessons and I was proud that I could make a beautiful gathered cotton skirt. Secretly I dreamed that mom would sew something pretty for me, but she was too busy making her opera costumes and clothes for Sandy, who was too young to make her own.

As strange as things might have seemed around our house, there were good days, too. Some of the craziness even had payoffs. The Hudson, for example, really turned out great. Dad and I sold it at the end of the school year, and I got to keep the money. Dad wanted me to understand the value of a dollar and how dollars can be earned. I got the message – and the money – but hated working on that car and being treated like a boy almost as much as I hated being treated like a real woman.

Mother's opera career progressed and she became the lead soprano for the Santa Monica Civic Light Opera Association. Dad sometimes had singing parts and often Sandy and I were on stage as "spear carriers." We had fun performing our small silent parts. Mom was Gilda in Verdi's *Rigoletto* and Musetta in *La Boheme.* She sang like an angel!

Being in opera was almost overwhelming, especially the tragic operas when Mom had to die on stage. The worst was the impassioned death scene in *Rigoletto* with its crashing cymbals and wailing violins, which helped her hit a C sharp in a difficult aria. It was intense when the stage darkened as she sang her last note and breathed her last breath.

But how wonderfully beautiful she looked up there under the klieg lights, radiant in her rich brocades and satin, her blond good looks dazzling the eager hordes. The star!

Later, after an eternity of curtain calls and armloads of long-stemmed red roses, Sandy and I would hang around her dressing room while she was taking off the heavy stage makeup. Her opera friends whirled around her, enamored with her talent, hoping some of her glamour would rub off on them. Some were like aging opera groupies. Eventually their commotion would wind down and their attention would turn to her two little daughters who stood quietly in the shadows. They pinched our cheeks and clucked appreciatively over us, but no one ever really took the time to get to know us.

Besides becoming an opera extra, an auto mechanic and a real woman in fifth grade, I also became a swimming enthusiast.

My dad bought our family a brand new 14-foot house trailer which we left all winter in a trailer park near Palm Springs. It was there that I perfected my swimming ability in the warm pool.

Compared with the rest of my life, the time in the desert was wonderful. My parents seemed to like each other better out there, so I was happy. Still I worried a lot about their getting a divorce. A few years earlier, after one of their ugliest fights, I made Daddy promise that he would never divorce Mommy. He cuddled me and promised, "Donnie, I will never leave your mother, and I certainly will never leave you." I knew he would never leave me.

Once before, when I was in third grade, they separated for a short time. Dad rented an apartment, moved me in with him and called me "the lady of the house," I hated that. It was hard trying to cook dinner and I missed Mommy and Sandy. So I was very much relieved when my parents got back together and seemed happy with each other.

On the way home from these idyllic weekends at the trailer, we'd drive down the Hollywood Freeway through Los Angeles, listening to the Jack Benny Show or George Burns and Gracie Allen on the radio. I would lay my head in my mother's lap while she stroked my forehead and I'd daydream, sun-burned, tired and happy from the swimming in the sun. I dreamed of that wonderful pool.

I liked to feel my mother's cool fingers against my sun-burned brow. It felt so nice. What would I be when I grew up? Would I be a radio celebrity like Gracie Allen? No, she acted too dumb. A pharmacist like Big Ray's mother, Lydia? Maybe. A mother? Yes, I would be a mother. Maybe a famous swimmer like Esther Williams...I drifted to sleep, smiling contentedly, visualizing all the laps I had done in the swimming pool.

Spring 1954
Culver City

Dad began to teach Sandy and me his distorted view of the world very early, attempting to shape our beliefs about the meaning of life and women's place in it to suit his own purposes.

It began when Dad taught us about Darwin and evolution. We took field trips to the Museum of Natural History to see fossils. We saw ape-like Cro-Magnon men and women and compared their skulls with the skills of modern people. Dad explained that human beings were simply animals who had not evolved far from the cave.

"I decided long ago to allow myself anything that dogs do," he told me more than once.

Exhibits showing the life of frogs, from their tadpole beginnings to their walk on land, were clear evidence of how things evolved. I was fascinated with the lungfish, which made itself a papery cocoon for the dry season. It would lie still in the cocoon, breathing through a lung-like structure, until the rainy season returned. Then when a lake formed on top, it would be set free. I often thought about that little fish. Perhaps I, too, could be set free some day if I could just keep still long enough.

We went to the La Brea Tar Pits near Maymie and Big Ray's house and saw bones of dinosaurs that had roamed through their neighborhood long before there were people on earth. By the age of ten I was proud to be an expert on evolution, and convinced that humans were merely animals at the top of the evolutionary ladder.

After we learned about evolution, our lessons began in earnest. While Mom was at opera rehearsal several nights each week, Dad taught us that there was no God. He read Robert Ingersoll's arguments against the possibility of a Supreme Being and expected us to discuss and support them with our own thinking in the nights to follow. It seemed logical to me. Indeed, how could there be a God? I could not see God.

Then came Bible lessons. Dad told us how ridiculous it was to believe God created the Earth and its inhabitants in six days – after all, we already knew about evolution. And how could those old Biblical heroes live for centuries begetting all those offspring? And what about a talking serpent? How dumb!

Dad explained that religion was to keep the miserable, ignorant lower classes in line; it was the "opiate of the masses." Of course I could not know he was quoting Karl Marx. He never let us forget that Mom's grandfather had been an Evangelical minister, which proved the ignorance of her family.

Then Dad would turn right around and teach us the Ten Commandments, stressing, "Honor thy father." He told us that Eve was created from Adam's rib and her purpose was to serve Adam. Sandy and I learned that women were inferior and that we were on earth for the convenience of men. We were to understand that we were "lucky to be alive," especially me. He told me over and over that my mom's parents wanted her to get an abortion when she was pregnant with me because she was so young, but he had fought and saved me. I owed him my life.

Our lessons went on for years. Besides learning that the world's religions and values were nonsense, we heard in great detail about South Sea Islanders who were superior to us because they did not subscribe to incest taboos. Dad explained that it was necessary to teach young female children of the tribe all about sexual practices so they would be good wives. He taught us that it was necessary for girls to make themselves worthy of men. He even read us the passage in the Bible over and over about daughters who filled the father with wine and lay with him to save his seed.

*My father controlled our bodies, minds and spirits. As our primary caretaker, he gave us intense affection, but it was combined with brainwashing, abuse and the strict admonition to **never tell**. We lived in fear, under threat of violence. We never knew what form it would take - outburst of rage, bent-back wrists, abandonment outside in the darkness. We were so ashamed, how could we ever tell anyone what was happening to us? How could we even talk about it with each other? Besides, who would want to help us when we were so dirty, different and disgusting? No, his authority over our lives was complete. There was no higher power.*

I wanted so desperately just to be a dear little girl like my friends; to have my parents love me and take care of me. So I pretended everything was all right, even though Dad was always taking me off alone, away from Mom and Sandy.

Spring 1955
Culver City

"I can't take it any longer, Ray," Mom said through her tears. "I'm leaving. I'll get an apartment and take the girls with me. You can have Bernie and Cee Cee."

"You can move out for all I care, but Donnie and Sandy are staying with me," Dad thundered back at her. "And quit that sniveling."

I hated it when Mom cried. It made me feel powerless so I just cowered down in the corner of the back seat. We had just turned into our driveway and the car was stopped, but I was too afraid to get out.

Dad was just getting wound up. "I've told you what will happen if you buck me on this," he shouted. "It will be over – your career, your little romance. It's all over if you go against me. Not only that, I will see that your fuckin' boyfriend loses his cushy job, too. I've already hired the best attorney in L.A., and if you want a fight, I'll give you one you'll never forget. I'll have your little ass in a sling."

Mom dissolved into sobs as Dad went on, his voice an octave lower. "I'll take Donnie and Sandy out of the state," he snarled. "You'll never see them again."

From my vantage point in the back seat I could see Mom shrink up against the door of the car, her determination stripped away. Tears pouring down my cheeks, too, but I didn't dare do anything to stop the fight. I only hoped that Mom wouldn't go.

But finally, she did. Before she left, she explained how much she loved Sandy and me but could not stand Dad's insistence on having Bernie and Cee Cee. She told me she had a room for us girls in her new apartment and hoped we would come over often. She'd rented right across the street from our junior high to make it easy for us to see her. I had helped her find the apartment, but all along I kept reassuring myself that she would not really go. There was still time for her to change her mind.

I was frightened and ashamed about our family's breaking up but would not have dreamed of telling her. Instead, I did my best to comfort her. She always seemed unhappy and I never wanted to add to that. My role was not to make waves.

"Don't worry, Mommy," I reassured her. "Sandy and I will be alright."

"Are you sure, Donnie?" she asked over and over as if she needed permission.

I put on my best adult act for her. "Of course, Mom. You know I can cook and clean. And we can see you after school. It will be just fine."

I told her this, but I wasn't sure at all. How could I get along without her? How could she leave me?

The last day Mom ever lived with us inevitably arrived and it was awful. I awoke with my stomach in a tight clump, remembering this was the last morning we would ever be a family. I took a deep breath, put on a happy face and went out to the kitchen where she was packing boxes.

"Oh, Donnie, I'm glad you are up." She sparkled with excitement. I could feel a new aura of energy around her.

"Good morning, Mom. So this is the big day." I used my cheery grown-up voice to conceal how scared I felt.

"Would you hurry and get dressed? The movers will be here around noon and I still have so many boxes to pack. Would you be a dear and pitch in?"

"Yeah, sure," I mumbled, aware that my bravado was slipping. Helping her pack was the last thing in the world I wanted to do. In my heart I wished she would unpack everything and stay. I took one last look around before everything changed. The old-fashioned upright piano Mom had inherited from her mother was flanked by a green print sofa and our new black-and-white TV set. Dad's green plastic lounge chair stood on a pretty wool area rug.

The kitchen was cheery and clean, a pretty blue room that Mom had painted. She had selected a darker blue for the spindly chairs and table from a secondhand store, creating the illusion of a set. I had been comfortable in this little house – it was so much homier than our other place at the beach. Now what would happen? Sandy and I were used to taking care of ourselves, but with Mom leaving to start her new life, who would make us beautiful Easter baskets? Give us hugs?

I couldn't blame her for leaving Dad, though. I was old enough to understand why she couldn't stand having Bernie around because she was always getting pregnant. I remembered how upset Mom had been the night Bernie flopped down on our green sofa just a year before, huge with another baby, telling Dad it was time. She and Dad left together and came back a few days later without the baby. They said it was a beautiful baby boy and they'd given him up for adoption. I wondered whether they would have given the baby away had it been another girl put on this earth to serve men. And I always wondered where my baby brother might be.

Then a few months later Bernie got pregnant again. This time Dad and Sandy drove her to Tiajuana for an abortion. They brought her back to our house and I put fresh sheets on the couch so Bernie could sleep there for a few days to recuperate. Mom was furious with Dad that time and screamed about Bernie's bleeding on our couch.

But the worst fight they ever had was when Mom's diaphragm was missing. She told me the story over and over again, apparently having trouble believing it herself.

"Donnie, when I asked your dad where it was, he just looked at me with an insolent smile on his face. All he could say was, 'Well, you didn't want me to get Bernie pregnant again, did you?' I don't know how I'll ever forgive him."

I brought my mind back to the present and began to help Mom pack. I never knew what to do about the problems my parents had – there was no way to help.

The movers came and loaded everything onto the van except Dad's green chair, the TV set and our beds and dresser. We could hear our voices echoing around the empty rooms. Mom went off to start her new life and after she left, my heart felt empty, too. Deep inside I was afraid of living with Dad without Mom around.

In the year after Mom's move, Sandy and I used to sit together in the big green lounge chair watching the Mouseketeers and waiting for Dad. He had a job as a design engineer now with an aerospace company down in El Segundo, and even though he always got home promptly at 5:30, the afternoon stretched out endlessly. Mom lived close to our school but it was a long bus ride from our house so we didn't see her very often.

I decided to cover up my embarrassment about my parents' divorce by not telling anyone. I knew I could keep this secret – it was just another secret, another part of me I could never share with anyone. If people knew the real truth about me, I knew I'd never have a single friend.

I was especially careful to keep the truth from Leanne. Her friendship meant so much to me. I don't think I would have done so well without the fun, companionship and protection she offered me, and the safe oasis of her home.

I spent at least two nights a week with Leanne, mostly at her house. Once, when I accidentally broke a Johnny Mathis album belonging to a friend of her mother's, Leanne saw how frightened I was and decided to take the blame herself. I was amazed to find that someone cared enough to stand up for me.

"What can they do to me?" she asked. She was confident and bold.

I was startled at the question. She wasn't afraid of punishment at all, but I knew so much about it that it petrified me. We ended up paying for the record but we were not really in trouble. Leanne's mother was understanding and treated us like responsible human beings. I decided that if I ever had children, I wanted to be just like Leanne's mother.

Leanne and I became the closest of friends and as we rounded that difficult corner into adolescence, we shared secrets – at least Leanne told me all of her secrets. She was sensitive and tender-hearted, loving and good, and cried more easily than I. But then I seldom cried at all. I longed to tell her everything but I knew how serious my secrets were.

We did talk about boys, though. That was the most exciting topic of all! We discussed who was "cute" and how exciting it would be to wear one-inch heels at junior high graduation. We could hardly wait. As our girlish giggles and guesses about boys, kissing and dating inevitably became more grown-up, I pretended to be just as innocent as she was. I had to be very careful to follow her lead so I would sound like a normal adolescent.

On July 15, Leanne and I went with her parents to spend a week with friends of theirs down on the Palos Verdes peninsula. It was beautiful there in the hills overlooking the Pacific. However, there wasn't much for us girls to do, so our host, who was a Boy Scout leader, invited his whole troop over to meet us. Leanne and I were beside ourselves, nervous and giggly all day. A whole troop of boys coming to meet us!

One by one they arrived. One in particular, Kenny Friess, was very special. I was drawn to him the moment I saw his handsome face and solid body through the glass of the door. He was dressed immaculately in a fresh white button-down shirt and dark cotton slacks and had a short up-to-the-minute haircut. I was usually talkative and funny, but suddenly got silent with this serious-minded boy. My mouth went dry, my face felt hot, and I worried that he might not like me. What if he could tell what my father did to me? That I didn't have a normal family? I couldn't bear it if he thought I was awful. He was the most handsome boy I had ever seen.

We all had a pleasant afternoon drinking Cokes and getting to know one another. That night when I was alone with Leanne, I spun around and around and flopped on the bed.

"Lee, isn't he cute? Did you notice how strong his arms are? Wasn't he funny when he said, 'What are we all going to do? Just sit around and listen to each other breathe?' Wasn't he clever? Isn't he just adorable?"

"Donna, I've never seen you like this before." Leanne could hardly get a word in edgewise.

"He's so neat! I'm really shook." But Leanne wasn't listening any more. She had fallen asleep, leaving me with only a tank full of tropical fish to share my silent thoughts of Kenny Friess.

As the days went on my thoughts stayed focused on Ken. I could not eat or sleep. Our friend's mother noticed my condition and delighted in teasing, "The love bug's bitten you and you can't hold still."

I laughed with her hoping everyone would pass it off as some kid stuff. But I knew better, knew something powerful and real had happened in my life. It was scary and exhilarating. *And as it happened, I never did get over it.*

When we got back I could hardly wait to tell Dad.

"I'm going to die, Daddy! I know it. I'm so gone, I can't even eat!"

"Huh? Honey, slow down and tell me all about this boy. I couldn't get it all from your phone call the other night, you were talking so fast." Daddy's words were laced with curiosity and approval.

"Oh, Daddy! He is so cute!" My words danced out of me.

"So tell me! Tell me everything."

"Well, he is just so neato and perfect. The right everything. I love his arms. They are real muscley and he smells so good." I paused for a moment. "Maybe I could send him a funny birthday card or something."

Daddy smiled over at me. "Honey, you know they talk about puppy love and kind of make fun of kids and their crushes, but I fell crazy in love with your mother in the sixth grade. I think puppy love is very real."

I grinned at Daddy. "Do you really? You don't think I'm goofy? I feel silly being so excited about a boy I've only known for one week. Besides that, he shakes me up so much; I can hardly even talk to him. I think he's shy, too." I paused. "It's so fabulous to be alive."

"Donnie, trust your instincts. Do you feel all lightheaded? Does he make your breath go away?"

"Oh my gosh! I can't even breathe around him!"

"Just go slow, you have all the time in the world. Choosing a mate will be the most important decision you'll ever make."

"Oh, Daddy. I'm not even allowed to date for two years. I'm not looking for a husband!"

"You never know!" He turned to look at me. His eyes were serious. "Donnie, you are the single most wonderful thing that ever happened to me. I want the best for you. Now tell me all the rest." Daddy's voice was warm with enthusiasm. As I talked nonstop, he listened to every single word I had to say. Daddy made me feel very special at times like this, never young or silly. He had a way of showing me that my ideas mattered. He seemed as thrilled about Kenny as I was, and I was relieved that he didn't seem jealous.

It was always Dad who was so interested in my friends and what they were doing, in my assignments at school and my plans for my future. It was always Dad.

Spring 1956
Venice Beach

The year after Mom left, Dad and Sandy and I moved back to the beach house. The State of California had purchased our home in Culver City because they needed the land for the San Diego Freeway, which was about to be built right through our living room.

Once the three of us moved back to the beach, Daddy took time to give Sandy and me a lot of attention. He was concerned that we completed our homework, knew how machinery operated and how cultures evolved. There were wonderful days when his eyes shone with love for us. When he was happy, the whole world seemed to smile and I felt warm and safe.

When he was in a terrible mood, though, it was a very serious matter. To "cross him" as he like to put it, was for "sorry sisters," and the punishments were always more severe than the crime. To violate his routines or question his authority was to get into trouble. We had to wait on him without hesitation and follow his orders exactly. If he demanded a glass of water with cracked ice, we knew that water with uncracked ice cubes would be thrown back in our faces. When Dad told us to rub his back or draw his bath, we did as he asked. We knew that the bath water must be exactly the correct temperature or there would be a violent outburst. Once he threw a book and hit me in the eye. His rages were frequent and frightening. Then they'd subside and he'd be friendly again. We were kept off balance by his unpredictable Jekyll and Hyde personality.

He seemed to enjoy being a father and even liked cooking pots of spaghetti for our dinner night after night. We loved it when he made his specialty, mashed potato "ice cream" cones. At times, though, he'd be preoccupied, lying naked in his bed for hours with nothing but a sheet covering him, writing novels in longhand. He was writing a murder mystery and had certain books he referred to frequently. *"How To Commit Murder And Get Away With It"* was usually lying open at his side, and it had graphic pictures of mutilated bodies in it, which felt like an unspoken threat.

When I got frightened or angry, I'd try to remember how sweet he could be, like the time he got me my bike.

One Friday night I heard him calling my name before he even got into the house. He sounded very excited. I went running to the door, not sure what to expect.

"What is it, Dad?"

He was grinning. "See for yourself, Donnie."

He pointed to a bicycle propped against the wall of the house. It was a sleek racing bike with those thin tires.

"Daddy, oh, Daddy!" I squealed in disbelief. "Is this for me? My very own grown-up bike?"

"It's not yours yet, but it will be. Tomorrow I'm going to rig up the compressor and paint it so it will look brand new."

"What color, Dad?"

"Any color you like, Sweetheart. You've been talking about a big bike for a long time now and I want you to be happy with it. I'll paint it any color at all."

"Red! I want red!" I didn't have to think about it. This was the bike of my dreams.

"You got it." His smile came from deep in his heart as I threw my arms around his neck.

My shiny red bike was ready by Saturday noon and it was beautiful. I felt like a princess riding it up and down the street, and Dad enjoyed my riding it as much as I did.

Despite his many faults, he had that rare ability to play with children at their own level, and we had many good times. When he took us to Disneyland, he was nothing like those stodgy parents who browsed the shops. No, he went on every ride with us and had as much fun as we did. It got a little awkward as we got older and Sandy and I took our friends with us. We wanted to explore on our own and check out the boys, but I felt guilty if we did not include Dad. He seemed so lost if he could not go on the rides with us.

Summer 1956
Venice Beach

I had always taken day trips and weekend trips with Dad, but that summer after Mom left, we traveled even more. Maymie often came with us and helped pay the tab. I missed my grandfather a lot, but Maymie didn't seem to mind leaving him behind.

Even though I was too young to have a license, Dad insisted that I do a lot of the driving, and I enjoyed steering our new convertible down the highway, the breeze whipping through my hair. Sometimes he'd have Maymie drive and he'd pull me close to him under a blanket in the back seat, where he'd have his fly unzipped. I hated that! I was so embarrassed, I wanted to die. I thought I'd die if my grandmother saw my hand working under that blanket, if she knew. Part of me wished she would notice, stop the car, and insist that Dad stop it right now. But she never did. No one ever did.

We'd had a good two-week trip to the Seattle World's Fair, and I was at the wheel, driving south toward home, happily inhaling the rich scent of the forest as we approached Olympia, Washington. Dad, who was napping alone in back, muttered something about stopping at the brewery. Maymie and I looked at each other and decided to keep going. We had a standing rule that the driver was the boss of stops and breaks. But fifteen minutes past the brewery, Dad looked up, realized I had disobeyed him and all hell broke loose.

"Pull over, you shithead," he yelled at me. "I said to stop at the brewery."

I eased the car to a stop at the shoulder.

"Get out. Get in the back seat," he commanded in a rage.

I did as he ordered and Maymie got in the back with me, Dad took the wheel and angrily headed back to the brewery screaming and yelling all the way.

"I'm putting you on the next plane home. You are no good, you worthless piece of shit. You're not worth the time I spend on you. You disobedient little asshole, I'm not going to stand for this." There was no end to his fury.

"Now, Junior, you don't mean that," Maymie soothed, trying to rescue me from his verbal barrage. It did no good.

I cried quietly in Maymie's lap, my face buried in her soft cotton skirt.

As Dad pulled into the Olympia brewery, his mood shifted. We were going beer tasting.

"Cheer up!" he insisted brightly, the dark clouds of rage gone from his face.

I was furious but knew I must pretend to be over the humiliation he had piled on me, or I would be in deeper trouble. I stuffed my feelings, took a deep breath and pretended that I was okay. I often wondered how I managed to hide the hot coals of my anger, where it went to simmer quietly. Were there dark, smoldering recesses in my soul? It was a terrifying thought.

Dad used our tiny house trailer for our frequent automobile excursions. He would hitch the trailer to the back of the Ford and we would be off. Mostly it was the four of us, Maymie, Sandy, Dad and me. Sandy was a good driver, too, though she was even younger than I, and we could both maneuver the trailer around easily. I was in charge of cooking and could turn out a full meal in a matter of minutes. Maymie and Dad would rave about my breakfasts for miles, which made me feel proud.

These trips were Maymie's chance to teach us something about behaving like ladies, a cause that was very close to her heart. She helped Sandy and me dress up to attend high tea at the beautiful Empress Hotel in Victoria, British Columbia and took us to the legitimate theater where we saw Mary Martin swinging through the air as Peter Pan. Some of the greatest highlights of our youth were these motor trips and Maymie's treats.

Maymie was famous for her thrift, and Sandy and I laughed about her eccentricities. She was very well off but pinched every penny she could, even re-using Christmas cards by sticking labels over the signatures of last year's senders. Once she bought defective bargain gloves with no thumbs, and we giggled for months, whispering to each other that we must have a terrible birth defect because we were born with too many fingers. Maymie had given each of us a sterling silver antique spoon every Christmas, and when we elbowed each other and rolled our eyes about "another old spoon," she was quick to reassure us that someday we would thank her.

On our trips she made sure we understood their value. She took us to visit the most exclusive shops where she taught us about sterling silver patterns and the difference between England's bone china and fine French Limoges porcelain. She mesmerized me with her knowledge of beautiful things.

"Girls," she would begin, "You know that European monarchs were so desperate to own hard paste porcelain after Marco Polo brought it back from China in the late 1200s that they tried for 500 years to discover the secret Chinese formula. The English even used the ash from actual bones to create a type of fine china, which is why they call it bone china."

At other times she would tell us of elegant clothes.

"When I was about 14, your age, Donna, your grandfather bought me the most gorgeous white ermine coat you could ever imagine. I was the envy of my school chums in it. It held up wonderfully over the years."

Maymie had gumption. She was inspirational, educational, bold and fun. In our quiet times when it was just Maymie and me, she would talk about her childhood and describe lovely ladies in our family from another era, a time when gracious living was of paramount importance. Then she would mention the time she was sold, but I didn't understand what she meant.

Years later that kernel of information was to fall into place in a hideous puzzle that covered more than 100 years of history of the aristocratic Landis family.

Fall 1957
Venice High School

By the time high school started I was beginning to show characteristics of my future self. I had begun to blossom into womanhood. I'd had orthodontia and now had beautiful straight teeth. My blonde pony tail, smooth complexion, and newly developing figure made boys turn their heads. My confidence soared. I enrolled in the college prep courses at my father's direction and settled down in my classes determined to earn an A average.

Kenny and I stayed in touch, and he was on my mind all the time. We were too shy to talk to each other on the telephone, and too far apart to see each other easily, so we had to settle for a letter-writing friendship.

Leanne and I were still best friends and we ate lunch together every day with our group of friends from junior high. I was the only one taking college prep courses.

When Leanne's mother saw my list of classes, she discouraged me from taking them. She had convinced Leanne to take shorthand and insisted I have something practical, too. I stood up for myself. I was going to college. By now I was determined and was not going to waiver from my path.

When I turned fifteen-and-a-half, Dad gave me a one-year-old Ford Victoria. It was a dashing car, much more elaborate than many of my friends' parents' cars. It embarrassed me to drive it, especially with the fuss that my friends made to their own parents. Still, Dad insisted that I use it.

"Donnie, you need this car for your self-esteem. You've had some strange messages about who you are, living in beatnik Venice and coming from a divorce. You're the aristocracy and I don't want you to forget it. Yours is the nicest car in the whole family."

I soon found out, however, that this car, with its payments, insurance, and maintenance, was yet another way in which my father would control me. The car allowed me to pick up Sandy from junior high so that we could sell the remaining merchandise from our grandfather's pharmacy. The stock and fixtures were moved to a new location and we started a sundry store. My grandfather had finally retired to his checkers, and Sandy and I, at 14 and 15 years of age, were in charge.

Our new location in the heart of colorful, offbeat Venice attracted some strange characters. It was not unusual to look into the face of a long-haired, drugged-out man staring through the store windows at us. We learned quickly how to ignore these characters but it was still scary. We had no gun or protection of any kind and hoped to stay safe by perfecting an "all business" demeanor.

Sandy and I opened the store each day after school for the next two years. We sold sodas, newspapers, candies and what was left of the stock of stationery, cologne and over-the-counter remedies. Most days we had few customers. We made cheese sandwiches in the back room for dinner, then closed the store at 9:00 p.m., drove home and organized our clothes for the next day of school. I would fall asleep exhausted, praying to be left alone.

The hard work was not as bad as the low income, personal danger and the demanding schedule. Behind the counter of that store on summer Sundays, I wished with all my heart that I could be one of the carefree, happy beach-goers I saw driving down the street in their colorful convertibles.

Dad would tell us in his professorial tone how much we were learning from running the store.

"Do you realize, girls, that you are learning to manage a real retail operation? Do this right and you'll make big bucks; way more than someone in a stupid Junior Achievement program."

Sandy and I thought we were living a nightmare. The summer before, he had made us clear sand from the back of his new lot at the beach for six hours a day. We were small girls – I was only 5 foot 3 inches tall and weighed in at 120 pounds, and Sandy was smaller – but my biceps grew so large that the boys made fun of me, and I was furious when I saw a backhoe on a nearby lot move as much sand in an afternoon as we had moved all summer.

Now this year Dad decided we would begin actual construction on the oceanfront house which was to become our permanent home. The three of us would build it ourselves. Sandy and I had to jackhammer out the thick round pilings on the lot and pour the cement foundation into Dad's homemade forms. Crudely constructed, they practically exploded under the pressure of tons of liquid cement pumped into them, and we ended up using hundreds of pounds of cement more than we needed. It was a mess!

"Daddy, we need to talk to you," I said hesitantly. Sandy stood next to me, quietly, letting me take the lead.

"Daddy, this is just too much!" I insisted. "I go to school all day and it's hard for me this year, especially chemistry. I go pick up Sandy. I work in the store. I can't do all of this. I don't want to build the house!"

Caught up in my own argument, I continued, my confidence and determination growing. "I really want to spend time with Leanne, and Kenny keeps coming by the store on Sundays on his way to go surfing. He asked if I could go with him sometime.

My father just lay there, clenching his jaw as he often did when he was angry. Finally he spit out, "Are you defying me? We're going to damn well build this fucking house whether you like it or not. I've got too much money and time invested to let some chicken-livered kids stop me now. We're going to build this house and that's all there is to it."

His tone then changed from fury to sarcasm. "If you don't like it, you can leave right now. Do you have somewhere to go? How about moving in with your mother? All of you jammed into her one-bedroom apartment. She'd love that, wouldn't she? And you, young lady, could try walking again. What about college? Forget that! You'll have to work at J.C. Penney's."

I breathed deeply and tried to hold my ground. "It's too hard, Daddy. I can't do all of this. My throat is sore all the time. My tonsils always have white spots on them. I'm getting behind in chemistry."

He yelled and threatened some more, and in the end I had to give up. I could never win. In retribution he took away the Standard Oil credit card that I used to buy gas for all the errands he sent me on. He said that I would have to use my own money from now on. I never got the gas card back. Our punishment for challenging his authority was to have our labor tied into our pocketbooks. We were not allowed to work for anyone but the family. Our sporadic small allowances were now abolished, and extra cash for personal items disappeared. Now the only way to get money for clothes and necessities was to work for him.

We built that house, every square inch of it.

1958
Venice High School

I often came home from a study date in high school to find Dad waiting to rush me to the construction site to help him with something.

One night he'd found a plumbing leak and took me to the job site at 11:30 p.m. He needed two people to run the water. We did the plumbing tests, found several more leaks and spent the next few hours getting pipes ready for the inspector who was coming in the morning. There was no sleeping that night. I went home in the morning, cleaned up and went right to school.

My grandparents' beach house, which had no garage, did not have much storage for building materials. The tiny cottage was filled with a boxed toilet, sinks, a tub, pipes and pieces of metal. Dad's huge bed dominated the living room. Sandy and I had beds shoved into the corners. I knew that the house looked too weird to have anyone over.

It was during this time, while we were living at the beach house, that my father made me go into the bathroom with him. He locked the door behind us.

"No, Dad, no...," I protested.

"I just want to see you. To see if you have something," he responded.

"No!" I knew what this meant. I felt the fierce anger flood me.

This same conversation continued for several more minutes. Then he gave up. I couldn't believe he actually gave up. At first it seemed like a miracle. Then he handed me a paper bag containing a small bottle.

"Donnie, I'm so sorry, but you might have something called crabs. Here is the medicine to kill them if you do have them."

Horror filled me as it never had before. "Leave!" I yelled as I slammed the door to the bathroom shut again and locked myself in.

I sat on the floor, took off my Capri pants and my panties and examined my privates. They looked like little brown freckles, but they had legs. Legs! I thought I would die. I wanted to lock myself up in a closet or run away. I had always felt ugly and dirty and disgusting, but this was proof of it.

I hated my father at that moment, but I also depended on him for everything. I did not know what to do, so I turned the hate on myself. I prayed that I would magically disappear. I would just walk into the ocean and never come out. My chin began to quiver.

Then for the first time I felt a gentle voice coming from inside of me, silently saying, *You'll be okay. You'll be okay. Don't lose control.* I did not believe that voice. The quiver inside grew into a quake and a horrible cry escaped from me. I curled myself into a half-naked ball on the floor. My head was pushed between the toilet and the tub. The tears came then, the stored flood of a lifetime. I hurt so badly, way deep inside. I cried and it scared me to cry. I never cried. I wanted to die.

After a long time I sensed the same loving voice inside of me again: *Donna, you'll be all right. I'll take care of you.* It was soothing and gentle. Finally, my crying stopped.

Get up now, Donna. Get up. You'll be okay. I promise you...

As the weeks passed I applied the smelly purple medicine to the crabs. Eventually the infestation was dead, but pushing all of those powerful ugly feelings down was getting more difficult.

I wanted to get away from my father's house more than I wanted anything else in my life. Each lesson I learned, each paper I wrote, each exam I passed, brought me closer and closer to the day I would finally be free. That helped give me the determination to keep on working. I was not going to let my father ruin my life. Somehow it would become normal. The gentle voice inside kept telling me it would be all right, and I began to have faith in it. Perhaps it was actually faith in me.

Our house on Ocean Front Walk was finished at last and we moved in. Dad still had his bed in the living room but Sandy and I each had our own bedroom now. That didn't stop Dad from bothering me, though. If anything, he was at me more often, forcing his way into my bedroom at night. I would always feign sleep, and if that didn't work, I would kick and bite and try to fight him off. I bought a lock but he removed it. I never won a battle, but still I kept fighting, hoping he would leave me alone.

While he was making me feel filthy and bad at night, Dad never lost an opportunity to tell me how important it was to be a good girl where the boys were concerned.

I was not allowed to date until my 16th birthday and then only boys Dad approved of. There was a boy named Don in one of my classes whom I liked very much. He was bright and athletic-looking, and as the semester progressed, our friendship accelerated to the point where he asked me out. I was ecstatic! He was funny and handsome, and he liked me.

I had turned 16 at last and was finally invited on a date. I went home on cloud nine.

"Daddy, that boy in my Spanish class, Don, the one I like, asked me to go to the movies with him next Saturday night. I want to go, but I told him I would tell him tomorrow."

"Donnie, I've told you I don't want you going to those Venice High dances or going out with those boys," he reprimanded me.

"Dad, he's a nice boy. I've known him all year. We're just going to a movie," I pleaded.

"What does his dad do?" my father sneered.

"He is a heavy equipment operator. He works for the State, building freeways. Don has a nice car and nice clothes," I argued.

"Donna, I have told you hundreds of times. You are not going to go out with any boys who are going to be truck drivers. We are the gentry. You must only date boys who are going to college."

"Dad, he's a very nice boy. This is ridiculous!" My tone was angry. "I don't know any boys who are going to college. I like Don. I want to go out with him. It's only to the movies," I wailed.

"Absolutely not!"

"Why not?" I continued to argue. This was important to me. I could feel my temper rising to the surface. I knew his reasoning was not logical.

"Because he is not of your social class!" he countered.

"So what is so big about my social class? Is it this mansion we live in? Is it all the money you make? Is it your illegitimate child? Or Mom's job in the park? Or Bernie checking groceries at Safeway? Why do you think Don isn't good enough for me to go to the movies with?"

There was no reply. Dad stopped arguing and walked away. The discussion was over. Though I still was not permitted to go out with Don, I felt that I had somehow pushed Dad back.

There were many instances when he would not allow me to have my own feelings or control over my own life. I felt powerless, frustrated, and furious. My feelings were so strong, I was afraid of the anger I kept buried inside.

I had moments when I wished my father were dead. I shoved these intense feelings down, disgusting feelings I had about what Dad did to me and about those crabs, about all of it, since my memory began. My real thoughts and feelings were more than too horrible to deal with, so I pretended that I was okay.

Guilt overwhelmed me and I felt like a bad daughter when I let myself think that Dad was not the all-American good guy he pretended to be, the Dad everyone else believed he was. My mind would banish these bad thoughts and replace them with memories of all the time Dad spent teaching me and helping me with my homework. I thought of how caring and sweet he could be sometimes.

Who was I to question my father? I put on a bright smile, a positive attitude and counted my blessings. After all, I was healthy, attractive, intelligent, strong, capable, and adored by my whole family. I worked very hard to convince myself that this was all true.

To help compensate for my bad feelings, I demanded perfection from myself. I seldom missed a day of school, made sure that my papers were perfect, my grades were perfect, my behavior was perfect. Only when I was perfect did I feel acceptable.

Leanne's dad was part of my fantasy about having a normal family. He was the busy president of an aircraft factory and could spend far less time with his children than my dad, but I could tell that he was concerned about me. He seemed especially upset one day when I was leaving their house and the tire on my car went flat a few houses down the street. I went back and used their phone to call Dad for help. He berated me, "Jesus Christ, Donna. If you are going to have a goddam fucking car, you will damn well change the tire yourself."

"Yes, Daddy." I was so upset by his response that tears welled in my eyes, "Lee's dad is here and he'll help me change it. I'll be home in about 25 minutes."

"You will goddam well change it yourself. I will not have you inconveniencing Leanne's father because your tire is flat. You will change your own tire or you will walk, young lady. Don't you dare cross me on this!" He hung up.

The tears rolled down my face. Leanne and her parents had not seen me cry in the seven years they had known me. It was humiliating. What hurt just as much was the silent sympathy they showed me.

"C'mon troops!" Leanne's dad spoke up kindly, trying to change the mood. He steered the two of us out the front door.

"But Frank, my dad told me to change it myself. I know how. It's okay. I really only called him because I knew that I would be late. I didn't want to get into trouble."

"You're my other daughter, remember?" He walked us to the car, one hand affectionately guiding each of us by our necks. "It'll just take a few minutes. You can help." His tone was reassuring.

Frank changed the tire while Lee and I silently looked on. I knew that Leanne's father respected me. He often praised me for being a "good Joe." It was strange and wonderful to have him defy my dad to help and protect me. Yet the entire incident embarrassed me. For the first time, I knew they had glimpsed into the reality of my life.

September 1959
Santa Monica High School
Santa Monica, California

I transferred to Santa Monica High School where I entered as a junior. Sandy had just graduated from junior high and signed up at "Samohi," too.

Things were definitely looking up. I would finally be allowed to date and got to school parties. I joined a girl's service club and was instantly involved in a new life of friends and activities. The horrible recent burden of construction and carpentry had been lifted from our young shoulders.

Sandy and I did well in school. At home we did what we were told, ran the sundry store and always acted like young ladies, just as our father demanded. We worked very hard at being perfect, and in many ways we did very well indeed.

My grades allowed me to graduate a semester early and I was honored as a California Gold Sealbearer at graduation. I had earned an A average every semester of high school. For some students this award might have been expected, but for me it was a great achievement.

It was great, not only because I had so many other responsibilities, but because it showed me, for the first time in my life, that I could accomplish whatever I set out to do. It meant everything to me.

Fall 1960
Santa Monica City College
Santa Monica

After high school, my father decided I should attend Santa Monica City College, a junior college just a few miles from home. I had no idea that my grades qualified me for a scholarship to almost any university I could have chosen to attend. I worked hard at SMCC and became Associated Student Body Vice President, Miss Spindrift Princess, and Woman of the Year and was an honor student, while I worked 20 hours per week at a park teaching charm classes to young girls.

I kept dating Ken on and off, though the long distance we had to travel to see each other kept our romance cool. Ken was still the only boy I had ever really been in love with, but our inconsistent relationship kept me from letting my guard down. We both dated other people, and I wasn't really sure how he felt about me.

In spring of the next year when school was out, Maymie invited me to accompany her on a six-week tour of the South Pacific aboard the *Mariposa*, a luxury cruise liner. It was the best trip I had ever taken.

Before we left, Maymie sat me down for our "ground rules of the trip" talk.

"Dear, you know how people always take you for my daughter because you favor me so? Well, I want you to pretend to be my daughter, not my granddaughter. I just don't want to give away my age."

"But, Maymie, what if people ask about me? What do I say if they ask if I have a sister? Are you going to tell them that you have a son? Is Dad to be my brother?" I felt overwhelmed by the deceit. What if Big Ray found out? How many secrets did my family have to have anyway?

"People don't ask that many questions. Just follow my lead. You will be my only child."

I knew that we would be dining with the same eight people for all our meals during the six-week trip. I paused as the enormity of trying to keep this secret sank into my brain. What if I slipped up? Six weeks was a long time.

"It seems like they will still want to know about us. What if they ask about our family? What am I to say?"

"It won't be a problem. Just follow my lead and smile a lot," she concluded.

She was right. It was no problem at all. I had been so well-schooled in the art of pretending, I could carry off our little charade easily.

My grandmother loved to dance, so did I, and we became known as "the dancing Landises." The cruise ship was filled with older, retired travelers, so my young-looking grandmother and I especially enjoyed the attentions of the ship's officers and other passengers. As a young single woman, I was bombarded with attention. I won dance contests and costume parades, swam, studied, played and attended ship style horse races. What a memorable trip!

During the cruise I saw the adult world from a new perspective. This was the first time I was included in adult activities as an equal, and it was shocking when one of the middle-aged ship's officers told me in some detail about his vasectomy. It did not take much sophistication on my part to understand where the conversation was headed. Later that evening he asked if I would some see his exotic fish in his state room. I just smiled and said no. Later I saw him leave with an attractive middle-aged woman. I had talked to her on deck and knew she was married.

The adult world seemed to be fueled by a free flow of alcohol. By the fourth week at sea, I had become fairly good friends with the women at our table. For weeks they had made jokes about alcohol. In fact they started a chant which they repeated before dinner, while the champagne was poured: "Alcohol's the only way!" I frequently visited with them during the day in the library or around the swimming pool. On one particular evening, our table companions held a pre-dinner cocktail party that Maymie and I attended. We left early, but they all continued to drink. By the time they arrived at our round table in the formal dining room, they were all quite inebriated. Tom, the ship's first officer, and perhaps the most dashing and handsome older man I had ever seen, bobbed his head against his chest, barely able to mutter. Nan, my friend in her 60s, was seated next to me.

After the appetizer and cold soup, Nan's head slumped toward her plate. Her husband, unsteady himself, took her to their stateroom. An officer from an adjoining table came over and helped Tom to his cabin.

Perhaps this was just a typical moment in shipboard life, but it was quite significant to me. I had never seen people out of control like this. Drunk. The respect and admiration I held for Tom and Nan and the others diminished considerably after that night, and they seemed embarrassed to be around Maymie and me as well. Somehow, their jokes about "alcohol's the only way" seemed sadly pathetic and hollow to me. That incident caused me to examine my life and what I wanted out of it even more closely.

I did not want to be 60 and dependent on alcohol to have a good time. I never wanted my head to fall into my plate. I did not want to be married to a man like these men. They had a great deal of trouble relaxing, were impatient for the trip to be over and seemed somehow dissatisfied within themselves.

My ideas about the kind of life I wanted to carve out for myself were becoming even clearer to me, and I began to miss Ken. I'd had a big argument with him before I left on the cruise, and there had been no mail from him waiting at our ports of call. As the days went by, however, I began to look forward to seeing him when our ship returned to Los Angeles.

Summer 1961
Eagle Rock, California

Ken was glad when I got back, and we began to see more of each other. By the end of summer we were becoming serious. He was treating me like somebody special, and I knew I was in love with him.

I remember one of our dates when I drove to Eagle Rock were Ken was painting houses for the summer. I had borrowed a colorful pants outfit from Mom. It was terrific with my summer tan.

When I arrived at Ken's modest apartment, we greeted each other with a companionable hug. I could tell right away from his expression that he liked what he saw. I did, too. He was freshly showered and smelled wonderfully of soap and after-shave. Ken was always neat and clean about his person and his surroundings, and I admired that.

"What smells so good?" I asked, poking around the stove.

"Ah ha! That eez for me to know and for you to find out!" He teased in a pitiful imitation Italian accent. "Nothing is too good for milady. I have prepared un spineech soouffle and roasted cheeken for you," he concluded, mixing his French and Italian accents. He smiled at me in his curiously serious manner. Even when he joked, there was a solemn flavor to it.

"Kenny, dare I look into the refrigerator?" I teased, remembering the dead cat that had resided there the entire school year before. It had been his anatomy project, part of a lab requirement for that particular course.

"Ah, my dear. Anything that you please. Tonight zee feline eez not part of dee dinna menu. So sorry." He had now mixed Chinese with his French and Italian accents.

I laughed. I was so in love with him, I thought he looked more handsome than ever. Tanned from his outdoor painting job, his heavily muscled arms were covered with sun bleached hair. He worked diligently to prepare our meal as I set the table. We ate in relative quiet, each of use enjoying the companionship.

Later that evening Ken took me for a walk under the stars of the warm California night. It was fantastically romantic. We hiked the short distance to his college's amphitheater.

We sat on the cement steps, high at the top of the outdoor theater, talked about our future and resumed one of our favorite pastimes, imagining our future children. We dreamed about taking them on the merry-go-round at the Griffith Park Zoo. Ken cuddled me in his arms. I adored him and knew that he cared for me. It was wonderful to be together this starry night.

After our return walk, we lay quietly on his sofa and held each other. We looked long into each other's eyes. I kissed Ken's face a thousand times with tiny kisses. I kissed his closed eye lids, his ears, his forehead. We held each other as if we could never let go.

We never said so, but we both knew that we wanted more. I held back, always, because I knew that I wanted this "nice" boy, and I wanted to be the kind of girl that he would marry. The hours flew by, and before we knew it, it was time to leave. As I drove the hour home to Venice, my thoughts were filled with Ken. I wanted him as a woman wants the man she hopes someday to marry.

I pulled my car into the driveway and looked carefully around before I got out of the car. This was Venice and it was dangerous. At the door of the house, I put the key into the lock quietly, ever so quietly, and opened the door. I did not want to awaken Dad. I silently tiptoed three steps.

"Donnie!"

Damn! I ignored him. I just wanted to go to bed with thoughts of my dearest, wonderful Kenny.

"Donnie!"

I continued to ignore Dad's call from the dark living room.

"Donnie!" Finally, he got up. He was nude, as always. I grunted an unfriendly hello. He reached out to touch me. I pulled angrily away, my mood changing instantly.

"No! I have to go to bed!" My tone was fierce. "I have to get up in the morning. I have to be at work in six hours."

He reached for me again. I pulled away, defiantly on guard. He used his authoritative tone which I hated.

"I need you to take care of me!"

"No, no, no!" I whispered harshly, desperate to be left alone.

"Just help me!" He pleaded, trying a different tack. He went from begging to threatening to hissing.

This went on for a very long time. He would not leave me alone. I had to get some sleep. I had to be at work the next morning.

Oh, dear God, if you are there, please hear me. I prayed. *Oh, dear God, please help me. I need your help.*

My prayers and arguments did no good. He had been waiting for me, knowing that I had a date with Ken. It seemed to excite him knowing I had been out with my boyfriend. He kept after me, ordering, cajoling, begging and pleading with me.

"No, Daddy, no!" I argued back, I was crying now. "Oh, God, Dad, please leave me alone! I want to be normal. I want to be with Ken. I love Ken."

Still he would not stop. I usually tuned out when he grabbed me and recited to myself his familiar refrain – nice girls respect their dads, nice girls do what they are told. But tonight I was too angry to let him have his way.

Finally, he realized I was not responding to his demands, and he grabbed my right wrist and twisted, his special twist that left no marks. Pain shot thought my body. I hated him that night more than I had ever hated him in my life! I was powerless to stop him and I despised him for that, but I would not let him touch my body the way he wanted to. A small victory.

I had to "help him" as he so euphemistically put it. I separated my mind from my left hand. I did the dirty work while I took myself far away where it was safe, to my dream place, where I was normal and everything was finally okay. I dreamed that I would be set free.

September 1962
"The Row" – 28th Street
University of Southern California
Los Angeles

I graduated from Santa Monica City College
with honors and an academic scholarship to the
prestigious University of Southern California. The
combination of my scholarship and money I earned at
my recreation job gave me enough to afford the luxury
of belonging to a sorority, an opportunity that
changed my life. My new "sisters" were warm,
helpful and very funny.

Each day when I visited the beautiful colonial
home that was our sorority house, my dreams
flourished. I often dreamed of what it would be like to
live there. About six weeks into the semester, when I
visited my new friend Patty's room, I noticed that the
cupboards on the side wall were empty.

"Why is Laura's cupboard empty?" I asked
Patty.

"Didn't you hear? Laura is sick again. She had
to drop out. Her mother came by this morning, took
her out of her classes, bundled up her stuff and they
left."

"How long will Laura be out?" I tried to sound
calm. But the whirling sound in my ears and the
sudden beating of my heart were deafening me.

"They don't know for sure; at least for the rest
of this semester."

"So Patty," I tried to appear casual as I asked,"
"Who's going to take her place for now?"

"Probably no one. All of the girls have dorm
contracts. They can't break them this late in the
semester."

"What if I could move in here?" I ventured in careful tones, suppressing my increasing excitement.

"Donna! Could you? I would die to have you with us. We could be the Five Musketeers. It would be great! I saw our alum advisor this morning. She's downstairs reconciling the house books. Go ask her! Go right now!"

That night, after getting the go-ahead from the advisor and finding out the exact amount that it would cost, I approached my father. Dad had made it clear that I was to live at home; I knew I would be in for a major battle.

When all of my high school honor society friends went "away to college" to Cornell, Purdue, Cal or Stanford, there was never a glimmer of hope for me. Never in all the years of talking about college did we discuss my living on campus. I knew I had to choose my words carefully, knew my speech to him must be the best that I had ever made because so much hinged on it. As a speech major, I had begun to learn the importance of audience analysis. I understood the art of persuasion.

I mulled over the problem all day. Never in my 19 years had I wanted anything as much as I wanted this. If I could live on campus, I would be free. It would be the equivalent of a golden emancipation. I decided to appeal to Dad's obsession with being a member of the aristocracy.

"Daddy, I had lunch at the house today." My tone was light. I adopted a casual air. This must not seem too important.

"It was real nice. Tasty goodies to fatten me up." I paused companionably. "When I was visiting Patty upstairs, I noticed that one of the girls had moved out. Laura, she's the pretty brunette you liked who lives in San Marino. Her mother took her home this morning."

I allowed a long silence to rest between my ideas. It was crucial that I handle this right. No rushes of excitement. Don't show too much feeling. I carried on about my new sisters. I mentioned the doctor's daughter, a sister's Hancock Park mansion and some details about another girl's dad who was a four-star general.

"I'm sure enjoying getting to know all of the girls. Dad, imagine if you had a daughter who lived in. A real sorority girl."

There was no response from Dad. He was in bed absently chewing ice. I was sitting on a chair nearby. I let more time pass.

"I bet Maymie would like it, too." I forced another pause. I looked at Dad. He seemed interested. Go on, but be careful, I thought to myself. His jaw isn't working. He's still listening.

"Dad, the advisor said the total cost is $50 a month. That includes food. It's as cheap as feeding me at home. And without that two-hour drive, I'd have more time to study. I'm making almost $50 a week at the park and with that scholarship…"

"I don't like that scholarship at all. They shouldn't give you a scholarship and then make you work for it. I could have easily sent you to USC myself if Maymie had not fucked up our money. Can you imagine some stupid broad charging around the world for a year in the middle of the worst depression this country has ever seen? I hope to Jesus that you'll never be a spendthrift like she is."

I sat quietly as he ranted on.

"I make good money. The aerospace industry is booming. There's a cry for good engineers across the county. Kennedy's gonna get an American on the moon. Mark my words, he'll do it. He may be a Mick bastard, and all those Kennedys are crooks, but he's right about the Space program. They'll need the best minds. I could name my price."

"Dad, I know. That gyroscope you have orbiting the moon is super stuff. Important stuff!"

Taking an opportunity to give Dad the credit I knew he was looking for, I continued with what I hoped would sound like gratitude and sincerity. "Daddy, that job at school is nothing. I just spend two hours a week filling out book requests for the English professors. They are so funny to listen to. They argue about the weirdest stuff. One professor was all shook up last week because someone had corrected the way he pronounced the word spelled k-i-l-n."

"Kill," Dad said proudly. "Silent n."

"Right, Dad, I'm glad you taught me the proper pronunciation of such tricky words. Anyway, this professor was flustered to think he might be wrong. Since he couldn't get anyone else to agree with him, he finally came to me, a student, and asked me. I said, 'Kill.' He stormed into his office then and didn't come out again while I was there."

Dad chewed on the ice I had carefully cracked for his Coca-Cola as he thought for a moment. His mood changed back to friendly.

"You know that Big Ray's mother, Lydia, and his sister, Fay, both got their pharmacy licenses. Fay went to college at USC in...probably 1902. Pretty impressive women for you to live up to. All professionals. Your mother's side isn't too shoddy either. Her sister Margie has her master's and is a college dean. You should be proud."

Minutes passed. I remained silent. I knew not to push too hard. I waited for what seemed an eternity. My trembling had almost subsided now. The conversation has calmed me some, but I could still feel the nervousness in my voice.

"So, Dad, what do you think?" I held my breath, forced myself to speak slowly. "Could I move in until Christmas vacation?" I'd really like to give it a try, 'til Laura comes back."

I breathed deeply, steadying myself for the verdict.

It was a yes! I was thrilled beyond belief.

I moved into the sorority the very next afternoon. My new roommates were ecstatic. Before the end of the fall semester, the girls had nominated me for their Sigma Chi sweetheart representative and their Helen of Troy candidate. They said they had to have a cute blue-eyed blond and I filled the bill exactly. I was so happy!

Trust in my gentle inner voice was beginning to grow. I began to really believe in those delicate whispers that had come to me in the most despairing moments, saying, *Donna, it will be okay.*

Life inside the sorority house was everything I had dreamed of and much more. The cook, Augustine, made me wonderful breakfasts and packed special surprises in my brown lunch bag for me to take to the park where I worked after school. The girls were funny to live with, sneaking cigarettes or swearing and telling off-color jokes. I did not understand at the time that it was only a slightly rebellious way for them to play; I was not about to join in their games. I had been taught that young ladies do not swear and I wanted to be a lady at all costs. I was reluctant to break any house rules, not wanting to jeopardize what I had become. More than that, I would not jeopardize my freedom.

With me out of the house, Dad abruptly married Bernie in the spring. At the same time, Sandy got into some kind of killer fight with Dad and mysteriously moved in with our mother. Sandy would not even discuss it with me. Wrapped up in my new life, I paid little attention. I was so thrilled to finally, joyfully, take charge of my own life.

It would be decades later before I learned the awful truth about why Sandy suddenly moved out of Dad's house in the middle of the night, never to return. I was to learn her story was much like my own.

September 1963
The Row
University of Southern California

I kept my engagement to Ken a secret from everyone, even Sandy, so that when school started again, I could participate in one of the oldest sorority rituals, "passing the candle."

It had been an incredible summer, a real roller coaster of emotions. Big Ray died and I was devastated, then there was the tremendous excitement of learning that Bernie and Dad were expecting a new baby, plus the most unbelievable of all! Ken asked me to marry him!

Thursday night was House Night and all 60 sisters ate in our dining room. All day long on that special Thursday I had been excited, my mind whirling nonstop. I thought about the night a month before when Ken proposed. He'd been so wonderful and so nervous.

After a nice quiet dinner for just the two of us, he sat me down. He was very serious. I was smiling; knowing what was coming and appreciating all the romance. He carefully bent his knee before me and looked into my eyes. In his earnest way he began.

"Donna, you know that I love you. You've known that since we were 15. I want you to be my wife. Will you marry me?" At that moment he produced the shining solitaire diamond ring which we had carefully shopped for together.

Laughing at how wonderful he was, like someone in a romantic movie, I threw my arms around his neck and hugged and kissed him. How I had waited for those words! It was like a dream come true.

"Yes, Kenny, I will marry you. And we'll have lots and lots of children! I love you. I always have, and I always will!"

Smiling, I brought myself back to the important matters at hand. Thrilling matters. I had ordered the traditional sorority engagement candle from the florist, a pink taper decorated with satin ribbons. I knew it would be beautiful. It would be delivered to the kitchen late that afternoon. I had been watching this ritual for a year now, every time one of the sisters became engaged or pinned. I knew what to expect and just how exciting it would be.

I had casually invited Sandy to dinner. She was living in Nichols Canyon now with Mom and Mom's new husband, Mac, and was always happy to come to the sorority house. During my classes that day I just couldn't settle down; I felt a magical electric charge course through my body every time I thought of the upcoming ceremony. It had been difficult keeping my engagement a secret, especially from Sandy.

At dinner, Sandy sat with me and Patty and my other roommates. Dinner went smoothly. Our conversation was animated, but I was waiting for dessert and what I knew would come next.

Suddenly, the dining room lights went out. They blinked off and on three long times. My heart was pounding. I gulped for air. One flash of light was for a pinning and three meant an engagement. The room instantly became silent, deafeningly silent. My heart was really thudding now. The girls looked from one to another. Who was it? The whispers quickly swept around the room. Names were tossed about excitedly. Everyone's curiosity was aroused. Just who could be engaged?

My name came up. "Donna?"

I smiled and shook my head no. Then I tried to put an indifferent, curious expression on my face that said I had no idea either. I had learned how to play the game.

A lean young waiter swept into the room carrying the most beautiful pink candle I had ever seen! It was burning and the satin ribbons flowed softly down around it. It looked like a fiery bouquet in the dim light of the dining room. The waiter carefully handed the burning candle and garland to the girl at the head of the table.

The candle circulated around the table, passing slowly from one expectant young woman to the next. With each pass, the intensity of the excitement grew. Sometimes a girl would bow her head as if to blow the candle out, but at the last instant would smile at her trick and pass it along.

Around and around the candle went. It came to me. I held my breath and kept my expression calm: I would not give myself away. I passed it on to Sandy. Her eyes sparkled in the light of the flame as she, too, passed the candle on. The candle went around to all 60 girls; still no one had claimed it. The intensity grew. This devious trick of not claiming it the first time was not new to the Alpha Gams. Every so often, a girl managed to hold on to her excitement and let suspense build.

The minutes ticked on. The candle found its way to me again. And again I did not betray the fact that it was mine. The tension in the room was literally breathtaking.

Finally, after one last round, the candle was heading toward me. I knew that I must claim it this time or it would burn down before it reached me again. It was now or never. My mouth went dry; my face shaded crimson. My heartbeat was so loud I could hardly concentrate. The candle was next to me now.

With a sharp intake of breath I received the candle in my trembling hands, and lifting it as if to pass it, satin ribbons swirling about, I quickly brought the flame toward my face and blew. The candle went out and the entire sorority house roared!

Sandy jumped out of her chair and shrieked as she threw her arms around my neck. "Sissy, you didn't tell me! When? When?"

I glowed back at her. The other girls were up and out of their chairs. Everyone was surrounding me, hugging me. My sisters were giddy, thrilled with innocent delight.

It was a moment I would never forget. I felt like a character in the fairy tales that my grandmother told me when I was little, a beautiful princess who lived in a storybook house and was about to marry a wonderful prince. It was beyond my imagination.

I really was going to be able to live the life I had dreamed about. Now I felt safe, accepted, loved and beautiful. My heart was filled with hope, wonderful blossoming hope.

Only faintly could I still feel for that little girl with the green teeth, the dirty neck and the feelings she had on May Day when no one would hold her hand.

June 20, 1964
Wedding Day
Palos Verdes, California

I awoke in the smartly furnished bedroom that Mom kept for Sandy and me when we visited her West Side home.

I dressed hurriedly, thinking of the stacks and stacks of wedding gifts displayed in fancy boxes from elegant stores. I had never dreamed we would get so many gifts. They had been arriving for weeks. My beautiful wedding dress was hanging from the closet door, billowing down to the floor. I had made it myself and was very proud of it. It was simple and elegant, and I was so pleased that Mom had made the veil and train for me after all those years of wanting her to make me a dress.

Daddy had given me only $300 for the entire wedding. He said any more would be a waste of money. My whole life he had told me about the days of wine, servants, free spending and about being the aristocracy. Then for my wedding he allotted me 10 percent of what my sorority sisters were paying for the same sized wedding. He was making good money, had new cars and was always taking trips. I pushed my frustration down.

For several weeks Mom and I had made finger sandwiches for 250 people in our spare time, carefully trimming the crusts, wrapping and freezing them. Katy, Ken's younger sister, had taken full charge of the wedding flowers. She had been so much help and seemed to understand about my limited finances. We'd finally chosen daisies because they cost the least.

Together Ken and I had saved about $1,000 and we painstakingly budgeted how to live on it. We figured out exactly how we could go to school full-time to work toward our master's degrees. It would be tight, but Ken's mom, Helene, was letting us have her family's cottage at the beach on Balboa Island rent-free for one year. If we were careful, we'd make it. But today was no day to worry about that. Today we're getting married!

Somehow we managed to get all the way to Saint Luke's Presbyterian Church in Rolling Hills on time. I was beyond excited. Though my stomach was in anxious coils, I kept smiling. In fact my face just smiled on its own.

I was putting the finishing touches on my makeup when Sandy poked her head into the dressing room from behind the closed door. "Donnie, Cee Cee and Leanne are all set and they look beautiful in the bridesmaids' dresses. Five minutes and we're on!" Her voice, charged with 100 volts, was much higher than normal. She looked beautiful in the yellow floor-length taffeta dress we had selected.

Daddy came in to check on me one last time. He looked more handsome than ever, too young to be giving a grown woman away. He was tanned and slim in his white dinner jacket, bow tie and cummerbund with contrasting black trousers.

"Donnie, how's my girl?" he asked, smiling comfortingly. "You're the most beautiful bride I've ever seen. I'm so proud of you for making that dress all by yourself."

"Daddy, I'm fine, but I'm shaking like a leaf. This is worse than giving a speech!"

"You'll be great. You always are. You're perfect. I'll meet you at the sanctuary doors in five minutes and we'll head down that aisle. You look wonderful. You're the classiest beauty I've ever seen! I'm so proud of Daddy's girl for landing such a great guy as Ken."

The familiar strains of "Here Comes the Bride" floated into my dressing room. My stomach lurched. One last look in the mirror. Wow, I thought, I really do look like a bride. The reflection showed a slim young woman, golden and gleaming, energy and vitality flowing from her. I smiled at myself and winked at Little Donna who lived behind that jubilant smile. Little Donna who had so dreamed of one day marrying a nice boy and living happily ever after.

"You did it, girl, all those semesters of studying all night, the only one awake in the entire sorority house. Earned your bachelor's degree last Saturday and with honors yet, and now this Saturday, a husband. You did great!"

My grin remained as I continued talking into the mirror, "Nothing will stop you now!"

I believed that comforting voice within that kept encouraging me. She had been right all along. I smiled goodbye to the girl in the mirror, the girl I had been. I took in a long deep breath and exhaled slowly as I turned and walked through the door to become the woman of my future.

Part II
Family Life

Fueled by love and ambition, Ken and I wasted no time making our lives work. During our first year of marriage, we completed our master's degrees and found good teaching jobs. Ricky, our first child, was conceived during our honeymoon year on Balboa Island. Our daughter, Julie, was born three years after Ricky came into the world; then three years later, Danny was born and our family was complete. We had the three wonderful children we'd always wanted.

We moved to a brand new house in Huntington Beach and were enjoying the wholesome suburban lifestyle. Our teaching schedules allowed us to indulge in our passion for boating, and we spent a lot of time moored in the harbor at Catalina Island.

In 1968, we bought a 43-foot Chris Craft with Maymie and Dad. Dad and Bernie's family grew as ours did. Before long there were too many playpens and cribs to make boating comfortable, so we sold the boat and Ken and I bought a mountain home near Big Bear. That added a new dimension to family life, and we were thrilled to be able to teach our children about the forest and the fun of skiing.

We invested in rental units and worked hard to build a substantial business. Between our teaching salaries and our investments, we were doing well. But for us everything paled next to our family life. Some people are more cut out for parenting than others, and Ken and I always knew that it was our true calling. We knew we were lucky to feel that way.

For the most part, Dad was supportive and we spoke on the phone almost daily. He seemed to have our best interest at heart, as he gave advice and encouragement. Predictably, life wasn't always a picnic with him, but we felt his genuine concern for our family, and he and Ken got along well enough. The situation deteriorated when he moved in with his girlfriend, Crystal and her daughter Jaime, while he was still married to Bernie. Bernie filed for divorce and Dad quit his job to avoid paying child support. The family was in an uproar. Maymie said she had never been so upset in her life, and Ken was furious because the situation forced us to help bail Dad out when the bank refused him a loan.

Our cabin in the woods was our saving grace and we spent every weekend of 1972-1973 up there fishing for German brown trout in the river, hiking in the woods and riding our Honda 90 dirt bikes over the hills. We picked apples in the orchard and made pies on the old black woodburning stove. It felt like heaven, and it was. In fact, we enjoyed the country so much that we decided to move our main residence from Huntington Beach to a rural area, further away from Dad.

San Juan Capistrano, where the swallows return each year to the old mission, was the most beautiful community we could imagine.

August 5, 1973
New Beginnings
San Juan Capistrano, California

"Kenny, be careful with the passenger side-view mirror. It's tilted down and you may not be able to see everything behind you. I'll follow right behind in the station wagon with Danny and Julie," I stopped, looked at my husband who seemed preoccupied.

I tried again, "Honey, are you sure you can really drive this thing? Have you ever operated such a big U-Haul?"

"I'll be fine, Donna. Just stay close behind me. It'll only take 40 minutes or so," He paused reflectively. "Just think, tonight we'll sleep in our dream house. Hard to believe, isn't it?" His voice was clear and deep and today there was excitement in it.

He walked over to the green 1972 Ford station wagon to check on our children. When he poked his head through the driver's window, our dogs, Ginger and Max, panting in the back seat, took it as a cue to wag their tails.

"Julie, Dan, are you all set? We're off to our new home; the place you'll always remember as the home where you grew up,"

"Daddy, I'm kinda hungry. I didn't like the stuff at Aunt Katy's for breakfast this morning," confided Julie, our five year old.

"Jugee, we'll take care of you. After we get the moving van to the new house, Mom'll get some burgers and drinks. Okay?"

Julie smiled her best smile, knowing that the next meal was not far away. Her big green eyes twinkled as she leaned back against the front seat. She was ready to go. Danny, our white-blond two-year-old, was secure in his blue vinyl car seat. He chewed his plastic GI Joe doll and smiled happily, sensing the excitement in the air.

I walked around the moving van and opened the passenger door. Rick was arranging some of the plants and more delicately packed boxes which were precariously jammed into the cab of the van.

"Rick, you all set?"

"Yeah, Mom. Let's go," replied our handsome eight-year-old son. "I can't wait to ride our new pony."

"I'm pretty excited, too, Ricky, thinking about having horses. Wasn't it great that those two Shetland ponies came with the house?" We held eye contact for a long minute "We'll go riding tomorrow." My heart pounded at the thought.

"Will you trust me with Weesha?" Rick asked, referring to our new Welsh pony.

When we'd bought Weesha, Ken had set me loose on her to try to learn how to ride. The only problem was she wasn't broken yet. "Your daddy is a nut, isn't he? An unbroken horse...an unbroken rider!"

"Mom, that just builds character!"

"Oh, so am I a character now, Ricker?"

"No, Mom you are the nut," he teased back. "You didn't have to try to break that horse; Dad could have done it first, then you."

"But that would have been too wimpy."

"But now you know how to ride. I'm impressed, but you can't have the Shetland because you won't fit."

Rick was chuckling. I guessed he was visualizing his mother standing with the pony under her.

I reached up as he offered his cheek, "Time to go, son." I pecked his cheek gently, "Bye."

"We're off!" I yelled, slamming Rick's door and running back to the station wagon.

I started the ignition. The sweet strains of "She's So Beautiful" came from the radio as I slowly pulled away from the curb.

I kept thinking about our new house. I had tried not to before the sale was final to protect myself from disappointment had the sellers backed out. But now I could allow myself to visualize my new life in vivid color. It was really our house now! I could get as excited as I pleased!

"And why shouldn't you feel that way, Donna?" asked my inner voice. *"You should be proud of what you have accomplished."*

I ran a mental checklist. It was a comforting rote for me. I had three beautiful children, a wonderful husband, a rewarding teaching career, lucrative investments, good health, a mountain cabin and now I could add "dream house" to the list.

No, I thought. This was not really my dream house. I have never dreamed of anything so elaborate. My dreams had always been grounded in practicality. Our new house had five bedrooms and sat atop two acres of land with gorgeous views that stretched forever. This house was Ken's dream. We were making a huge reach financially, but we both believed that we could do it.

I looked over at Julie, mesmerized by the drive past open range land and strawberry fields. Her face was turned away from me, but I could imagine her green eyes dancing with amazement. I smiled as I thought of another beginning: Julie's birth.

It was the only birth of the three in which I was able to participate without medication. I remember gasping and pushing with every fiber of my being, sweat pouring from my brow. Suddenly the pain fell away as my beautiful baby slipped from my womb. It was miraculous. Overcome with emotion I heard her lusty baby cry.

"It's a girl!" The doctor announced triumphantly.

"My dearest baby!" I strangled out as the tears poured. This was more emotion than I had ever felt before. Truly it was the most profound moment of my life. It was beyond words, a spiritual experience.

I was not prepared for it at all. No one had ever expressed to me what motherhood could be about, or life for that matter. I had been reared from the cold perspective of factual science. There had never been room for the spiritual. Spirituality was just something quaint to keep the masses in line.

But now I saw that was a lie! Suddenly I knew differently.

There had been dark years in my past, but what I felt at Julie's birth was a beacon of light filled with understanding and hope. I had used sheer strength of will and determination my whole life. I had always known that I was a survivor. I had always held on knowing that somehow, someday...

But I had never heard the rest of the sentence from my gentle inner voice. It had always just told me that it would be okay. Now I understood. The past was safely in the past. The horrible ugly years were all behind me now. I was safe.

I grasped something higher in that moment, knowing it would stay with me always. I felt connected to the immensity of the universe. I had a place in it and was part of a greater plan. Being a mother was more about reverence, commitment, dedication, and God to me than I could ever have imagined. I lost myself in those warm and alien thoughts. I also glimpsed something about God. Maybe God was in us?

I glanced briefly into the rearview mirror to check on Danny. He was still contentedly chewing on the GI Joe doll, a plump little toddler, sweet-natured and easy to care for. I remembered the day almost three years ago when Patty, my friend from college, had visited. We enjoyed trying to coordinate the births of our children.

That day I discovered that Patty had already started her third and I quickly decided that Kenny and I needed to add to our family, too. I called Ken at work and urged him to come home right away. We needed to get started so my teaching schedule would not get in the way.

Miraculously, two weeks later I knew that my mission had been accomplished. Dan was born in June exactly nine months later, and two days before Patty's boy. I could enjoy a whole summer at home with my new baby.

I checked the road ahead cautiously, needing to keep a safe distance behind the formidable U-Haul truck as it sailed southward. The new I-405 freeway allowed workers to commute from homes in the fast-growing areas of Mission Viejo, Laguna Hills and El Toro to metropolitan areas. Sleepy San Juan Capistrano was still rural and quiet. Horseback riders on the main street of the little town were a common sight.

Our new home would be more than a new house; it would be a new way of life. Ricky, my sensitive child, would be starting third grade and was anxious to get moved in so that he could look for yellow racers, his favorite snakes, in the riverbed.

When he was little, I was the only mother whose child demanded that she stay at all the birthday parties. There was a shy cord in me that felt as he did. It had taken all I had to force my way past that, to make myself who I was. But we did things at Rick's pace. I understood that when his time was right, he would take the world by himself.

I knew I was a lucky woman. Raising the children and having a family were the most exhilarating adventure of all. My eyes noted the freeway sign in front of me.

"San Juan Capistrano, Next Exit." Our friends thought we were crazy to accept a 70-mile commute just to live in the country. They also said we were lucky to afford such a home when we were so young.

Luck and grueling hard work was more accurate. We owned and managed 84 four-plex apartment units which formed our financial base, along with our two teaching jobs. We had made it the hard way. Our friends loved to hear our crazy landlord stories. They especially enjoyed the one about Ricky helping me paint an apartment. He caught his head in the rungs of a chair and I had to call the fire department to extricate him.

All those years of struggling were worth it now. It would be wonderful for our children to grow up in the open space of the 40-acre valley that lay at our feet. In the lush grove behind our house, Mexican braceros were picking fresh oranges. I could see their tall ladders leaning against the fruit-laden branches. The aroma of orange blossoms would fill the evenings.

I pulled into the driveway, set the parking brake, and turned off the engine. We were home.

Spring 1975
Swallow's Day Parade
San Juan Capistrano

In San Juan Capistrano one of our community rituals is the annual Swallow's Day Parade to celebrate the famous return of the swallows, "Las Golondrinas." This year our friends and neighbors decided that it would be fun to have a cross-country horse race after the parade. I had never really raced, and only had three years of riding experience, but with my usual enthusiasm I agreed to join the group and put up my entry money. There was to be a generous purse for the winner.

During the weeks approaching the big day, I took our horse, Windy, out for practice runs each afternoon when I returned from work. We ran the course and got in shape. On the day of the event, I was surprised to see dozens of horse trailers parked throughout our rural valley. Word of this race had really spread, and riders had trailered in their horses from as far as 60 miles away.

The three-mile course was marked, and men were stationed with walkie-talkies along its rock-strewn course. It was far more organized than I had imagined. Spectators were gathering along the course and finish line. I felt nervous and so did Windy.

What a mixed bag we riders were: middle-class businessmen turned weekend cowboys, construction workers who fancied themselves "real men," working cowboys from nearby ranches, local blacksmiths, stable owners, horse enthusiasts – and me, a school teacher who only rode bareback. I had
not mastered the saddle yet and hadn't really wanted to. I felt most comfortable bareback because I felt in control with my thighs pressed against the horse.

I could tell that our blacksmith, Joe, thought my entry in the race was the funniest thing of all. That school teacher? What a hilarious joke! He delighted in teasing me about it. I could just hear him laughing good naturedly, "Donna?" he would say in an amazed tone, and break up laughing. I didn't care. It would be fun. Besides I had never raced before.

As race time approached, all of us lined up at the starting line, perhaps 40 or more riders. My heart was pounding. Windy was shivering beneath me. I heard the starting gun and we were off!

Pressing my thighs tightly against Windy, we glided smoothly around the pack of riders as we headed into the riverbed. I knew that this was not unusual for Windy. She did not like to lose a race, not to anyone. She hated being in another horse's dust. We were racing like the wind, through rock and sand, past bamboo and bushes, up onto the dike that ran along the creek. We passed every one of the riders and were comfortably out in front when we approached the first lookout with his walkie-talkie carefully in hand. It was Joe. Later he said that he screamed into his walkie-talkie, "Jesus Christ, its Donna!!!" He was almost shocked speechless. He repeated that line many times that night at the post-race party. He could not believe his eyes.

Windy, pacing herself now, kept the lead as we continued across the course. Along the top of the dike, I leaned low against her neck. Finally a sharp turn back into the riverbed, where the trail was uneven with rocks and stones.

A horse could easily stumble and throw its rider off to be trampled by the pack of wild racers. The trail was much too narrow to avoid a catastrophe if someone fell. I was conscious of the danger, but I just kept crooning, "We can do it girl. Good Girl. Bring us in, Windy."

As we came into the final turn, I gave Windy one last kick and leaned down on her neck. As she turned the final corner I slipped and fell halfway off.

"No! Not now!" I said aloud. "We're so close." And then to myself, "You're almost in, Donna, hang on!"

I pulled hard, grasping at Windy's mane and managed to right myself. My friends were applauding and yelling. I crossed the finish line and the crowd roared.

I had won the race! I was the champion! No one could believe it. The school teacher! I was elated, but in my heart I always thought I might have a chance to surprise everyone. I had practiced ahead and put my mind to what I was doing. And I knew that deep inside I had a streak of daring. I had experienced that before. I knew what my horse could do, and I knew my own determination.

My friends were thrilled, but some of the macho cowboys were not. One man, Hoss, was so disgusted with his horse for not winning that he tied her up without walking her down. Unable to cool off as she needed to, she died a few hours later.

I knew this was a tough crowd, but that dead horse showed a callousness I didn't understand. Some of the cowboys were missing teeth and most of them chewed chaws of tobacco and spit the smelly wads onto the dusty ground. Perhaps that was partly why it was so intriguing. I got to go up against real cowboys and win. This outstanding day with Windy came to be, in some ways, a symbol for my life. It gave me courage, later, to remember I could win against all odds.

March 1978
Sandy's Home
Mission Viejo, California

My sister Sandy and I remained close during the years and she even moved to Laguna Niguel, fairly close to our house. She had become a dentist and had two darling daughters, Joanne, 7, and Mindy, 3.

One Saturday morning, I came to visit with her and her girls and go through some stuff our grandparents had left us.

"Well, shall we tackle that old box?" Sandy placed our coffee cups in the sink and steered me out of the kitchen door into the adjoining garage. I felt we were about to enter another world by opening up the box of our grandparents' memorabilia. I hoped it wasn't like Pandora's Box.

"Boy, Sissy, I don't know about this. Do you think it's going to bother us, going through May and Ray's old pictures?"

"I hope not. 1977 was horrible enough. This year has got to be better."

We both nodded in understanding. The year before had been horrendous. Our grandmother Maymie died, our mother was diagnosed with malignant melanoma, and our father got into terrible financial trouble.

"I think we'll be okay about all this. It's just old documents. Lots of pictures."

Sandy's head temporarily disappeared as she poked around the space above the rafters. Locating the box with her hand, she continued, "Dad doesn't seem quite as bothered now over Maymie's death as he was those first few months."

She lifted the huge brown carton down to me. "I couldn't believe how he stayed at Catalina on his boat all those weeks after she died. He has a little trouble with reality, doesn't he? He didn't remove any of her things from the house for six months. Weird."

I could visualize Maymie's silk slip as it had hung all those months over a chair, as if waiting for her to claim it. I'd often seen her put it on when she was dressing to go out. In my mind's eye I could see Maymie in her dancing gown.

"Do you remember Maymie's 75th birthday party? Do you remember what happened when she first arrived at my house?" I laughed. "It was so funny. At first I couldn't figure it out. Something was peculiar, but I couldn't put my finger on it. She was all dressed up. Then suddenly I realized she had her false eyelashes upside-down. They fanned down, forming a kind of bird cage over her eyes."

Sandy nodded her head. "I guess she figured that all of a sudden the world grew lines!"

"The really hard part was peeling them off her eyelids and gluing them on straight. I was laughing so hard inside that my hands shook."

We both chuckled affectionately at the picture of our little grandmother all dressed up with her upside-down eyelashes. We missed her.

"Sissy," I reminisced. "She did do some pretty strange things. Do you remember those gloves? The ones without thumbs? And the way we giggled about that for months?"

Sandy took up the litany, "And how we would start to imagine what odd-ball gifts she would find on sale for Christmas."

I continued, "I'll never forget the silver spoons. You'd watch me open mine, our eyes would meet knowingly, and in a serious voice, I would exclaim, 'Oh look, Sandy a new old spoon.'"

"Right!" Sandy's voice was filled with laughter. "We suppressed our giggles, but later we'd burst."

I returned to the present moment and looked at the dusty old box.

"How should we attack this project?" I asked, anxious to get it behind us.

"Well, we'll want an album for each of us, for sure. Cee Cee should have one and we should make one for Dad. The rest of the pictures can stay here until some of the kids are grown up enough to show interest."

"Yes, four albums will take long enough. But it does seem senseless to have more than 100 years of our family's life in a dusty box that no one can see."

For the next several hours we sorted through the box and studied ancient tintypes, report cards from the late 1800s, old documents, diplomas, and pharmacy licenses. We pieced together our family's history using these artifacts. Near the bottom of the box we found several bundles of postcards. Sandy lifted one of the stacks and untied it.

"Sis, these look real old. Maybe 1890s."

"They must be Big Ray's," I guessed as I reached for the other stack and began to shuffle through them.

I continued nonchalantly through the cards for the next few moments, remembering they always kept postcards from their travels. Usually they were marked with exotic stamps. I eyed these cards more closely. They weren't like the flowery old-fashioned cards I was used to seeing. I paused at one sepia-toned card: A beautiful little five-year-old girl smiled out at me. She titled her face adorably against her index fingers. She was beautiful. And she was nude.

I felt coldness spread across my chest. I rushed back through the cards, and stopped at a black and white photograph of a lovely two or three-year-old child. Her little dress carelessly falling off of one shoulder exposing her right nipple. I looked at the next one. This one was printed in German. It was a color picture of a little girl, maybe four years old, clad only in a garland of flowers around her bottom.

My heart was thumping and I was suddenly cold all over. The next card showed two girls lying in the forest. They were completely nude! I looked quickly at the next and the next and the next. Sirens began to go off in my mind. I hoped for some other explanation. Trying to conceal my frightening thoughts from my sister, I looked up at her. She seemed as shaken as I. A silent look of understanding passed between us, but we said nothing.

We efficiently rebound the cards and put them away. These were things of which we had never spoken and would never speak.

As I drove home from that visit, I was terrified of my thoughts. What does this mean? Not Big Ray? Not my beloved grandfather. He had never been anything but sweet and loving to Sandy and me. He had never touched me. He was not like Daddy! Was he?

More sirens went off in my head. I tried to quiet my mind, but it continued to grope for some understanding. What could those cards mean? I was certain that they were my grandfather's. They were a cherished collection, almost 100 years old, still bundled carefully, still in the family. They were once important to him. And perhaps to someone before him.

How much stress would my marriage take without falling apart? All of last year's problems crashed around in my mind. Maymie's death, my mom's cancer, the $20,000 loan Ken and I had been forced to pay off for my father. We had co-signed a note with him and he had defaulted on the loan. Ken was still furious about it. My mind went chattering on, but I managed to keep my eyes on the road.

The last few times I had driven alone in the mountains the thought of driving over the side had been painfully appealing. I tried not to allow these thoughts to continue because of my children, but they were real. I cut down on my speed as I reached our valley. Big Ray. What about my beloved grandfather? My years of talks with Maymie all came back.

Maymie always did her best to keep our family history alive and told me countless times of the successful Los Angeles family she had been born into. The memories kept rushing in, and I could hear my grandmother's sweet voice in my head.

"We've lived in the city for so many generations, we qualify for membership in the exclusive First Century Families of the Los Angeles club, and don't you forget it, Donna," she'd say.

One night after dinner at her house, while Big Ray read his newspapers in the living room, Maymie told me about her grandparents who had come out to California from the South.

"Donna, your ancestors were among the first settlers to come to America. Among them were signers of the Declaration of Independence. My mother's mother had her plantation overtaken by Union soldiers and had to cook for them. Do you remember when I told you about my great-grandparents both being suckled by slaves? Kat and William, my grandparents, moved out here with 11 children. My mother was one of them. Cousin Emily's mother was another. I've enjoyed a lifetime of being close to Emily. Real chums, more like sisters..."

Emily. That was it! Now I remembered what she had told me about Big Ray and Cousin Emily. She'd said she awakened in the night when they were all at Big Bear. She heard Big Ray with Emily. Emily was a teenager and Big Ray was in his forties. I did not understand what she meant at the time, but now I did.

Big Ray and Emily. Now it all made sense. My hands tightened on the steering wheel and I kept the car steady as random memories continued to fall into place. Shocking memories, tales my grandmother told in the nicest possible way. Did she know that one day I would piece them together and understand?

She loved to tell stories about the old days and she was good at it, too. She had majored in speech and drama at USC where, she never ceased to emphasize, John Wayne had been one of her classmates. But today, I could not have cared less about that old cowboy. Today, I saw Maymie again in my mind's eye, resting in her bed, on a day when I was young enough to be cleaning her house to earn extra money.

"Today, Donna, I want to tell you all about my mother. Cordelia was a wonderful woman, and I want you to hold her in your heart." I settled down at the foot of her big bed, comfortable in the folds of her blue down comforter.

"Everyone called my mother Delia for short," Maymie went on. "Delia married my father, Jonathan, a tile mason from Ventura. He looked a lot like your father, Donna. Perhaps it was Jon's remarkable blue eyes and handsome build that prompted Delia to marry him or perhaps Delia was pregnant. Whatever it was, it certainly wasn't his character. Delia definitely married beneath her. I always suspected a shot-gun wedding because he deserted us when I was four or five. Such topics were not discussed in polite society in those Victorian times."

"Anyway, abandoned by Jon, Delia struggled to raise my brother Phillip and me, and survived on donations and gifts from her wealthy sisters. She scrimped and managed to feed the three of us, but still we were poor, Donna. I remember my mother preparing a dinner for us three on one small can of Campbell's soup!"

"Delia was still husbandless in 1910 when she was friendly with the popular socialite, Fay Landis, whom she knew from high school. Fay was eagerly looking for a wife for her younger brother, Ray. She sort of courted Delia to encourage a match with Ray."

I had been a curious listener, sitting attentively as the tale went on.

"In private, Fay was having serious conversations with her father, Chadwick Landis, who later became the state senator from Los Angeles. Chadwick was concerned because his son was almost 30 years old and still had not found a wife. Ray was content with his studies of Latin, his checkers, chess, pharmacy business and the wonderful walnut ranch which he had recently purchased in Orange County. He had not gotten over the death of his mother, Lydia. She was only 43 when she died of cancer." Maymie's voice trailed off.

"Eventually Fay was successful at arranging a meeting between Ray and Delia. As a divorcee, Delia's marriage qualifications were not overly attractive for a man such as your grandfather, a man of wealth, education, and social position."

The storytelling stopped while we enjoyed dinner with my grandfather. Later during the dishes, Maymie continued. I noticed a certain pride in her tone.

"As I grew older Ray confessed to me that he never noticed Delia at all. He only had eyes for me. My name then was Gladys May and I was nine-years-old, hiding behind my mother's skirts. He described me as a little girl with long blonde ringlets flowing down my back. He said that he was struck by my blue eyes which he found fascinating because they slanted so. Anyway, he was not the tiniest bit interested in my mother. He wanted to marry me!"

I grew intent. Fay wanted Ray to marry Maymie's mother, not little Maymie...I was silent, uncertain what to say.

"Apparently there were some negotiations and he agreed to wait until I was seventeen before we'd marry. He also agreed to support my mother, brother and me. I was to go on little outings with him."

There was a long pause then. Maybe she was looking back over the years. Perhaps she was imagining her life with her mother and brother in some long-forgotten kitchen. Finally, in a far-off tone she concluded, "No one ever did ask me how I felt, but I didn't want us to keep getting by on that Campbell's soup."

I decided that customs must have been much different back then. Her girlhood seemed centuries in the past to me.

I had seen a sepia photo of her in a starched white dress at age ten. My grandfather stood close, a tall man in a dark fedora, vest, and a business suit with the gold chain of his pocket watch proudly displayed.

Maymie sighed. The far-away look was back in her eyes as she continued. "As Gladys May, I began going on outings with Mr. Landis. He seemed awfully old, but he was very nice to me. He encouraged me to change my name to the more stylish Vera-May, and bought me expensive clothes and jewelry. By the time I was 17, I had a huge diamond wedding ring, a large home, hired servants and the title of Mrs. Landis."

As I approached home, I realized what terrible evidence pointed to my grandfather. Big Ray *must* have been like Daddy. What an overwhelming revelation.

When I saw Ken's truck in the driveway, I knew I had to pull myself together fast so that he wouldn't know how upset I was. I tried to calm my mind and my emotions as the kids came running to greet me.

"Mommy, Mommy! Daddy's home early! Now we can go biking."

"Yes, guys. That's a nice idea." My cheerfulness was forced. I got out of the car and went in search of my husband.

With hose in hand, he was watering the vegetable garden and enjoying the beauty of the late spring afternoon. He was still dressed in slacks with the sleeves of his dress shirt rolled up. He looked so good to me. The children ran ahead, calling to him.

"Daddy! We want to go biking! You said we could!"

"Just let me change my clothes," he smiled, lifting Julie up and swinging her around.

Dan wrapped himself around his father's legs in his typical energetic greeting. Looking across the grass at me I walked slowly toward him, Ken greeted me.

"Sweet Patootee, you look about done in. Was that picture sorting rough?"

"Yeah, it was pretty bad. Made me miss May and Ray. It was kind of nasty," I offered, keeping the postcards and their horrible implications to myself.

"It wasn't just the pictures, was it? It's been a difficult year on all fronts," he consoled, giving me a hug with his free arm. The children ran to look at our new garden.

"I guess having your dad dump Bernie and the kids for that young gal, Crystal, and quitting his job to avoid paying child support has not helped matters. Borrowing money from us and messing up our credit got me all bent out of shape. I know that hasn't made it any easier for you."

I tilted my head back and focused on his face. He looked me in the eye, and when he spoke again his voice was softer.

"Donna, I'll back off. I shouldn't have ordered him to stay out of our house. I've been selfish. He shouldn't have defaulted on the loan, but after all he is your father. And I know I'm gone entirely too much, but you never complain." He paused, and after a long silence said, "Your dad can come around. I've been a jerk. I've been furious at him and you've been stuck in the middle."

Of course I hadn't complained, I thought, but this was no time to talk about it. I had other things on my mind. I remained silent for a long moment, trying to focus on Ken. My marriage was very important to me.

"Maybe we should talk about our ski trip," I said from my fold in his comforting arm. "It'll do us good to get away for a while. There's been so much happening." As we started toward the house to get ready for our bike ride, my mind still whirled with unspoken thoughts.

How could it be true? My darling grandfather with naked little girls? Maymie being sold to him. It didn't line up with my experience of Big Ray. But it made sense in a cold, logical way.

More pieces of the family puzzle were falling into place, and it wasn't a pretty picture. I stored it away in the back of my mind. I wasn't ready to deal with it then.

June 1978
San Juan Capistrano

"Mommy, it's such a warm day. Let's get Barbie a lemonade." Julie tugged at my arm, thrilled with her new Barbie Doll soda fountain.

"You pour and I'll be a customer, too." I was as happy as Julie was, home from school for the summer with plenty of time for the children. Julie was a wonderful playmate. Dressed in her white shorts and pink polka dot top, she still looked like a baby to me, although she was ten-years-old.

The afternoon wore on and soon it was time to put the toys away and start dinner. As we folded up the soda fountain, Julie tugged at my arm with an odd kind of urgency. I looked down and wondered what was wrong. She stood there with a pained expression on her face, her blond ballerina Barbie clutched in one hand.

"What is it, Julie? Does something hurt?" I sat on the floor beside her.

She had trouble speaking, but finally managed to whisper, "Grandpa…"

Our eyes met. Inside I went on red alert but managed to stay calm for her. "Go ahead, Honey. You can tell me."

She hesitated for another moment, and then blurted out, "He touched me."

Hot fury grabbed me and my temperature seemed to shoot through the roof. Then cold fear engulfed me. What more could I have done to keep her safe? I only left her with Dad in broad daylight. All the other kids were there, too, playing on the beach. I had just left for a few hours while I visited Mom and went to the mall. Just a few hours. I'd never left her when she was smaller.

I drew Julie to me and struggled to keep the alarm out of my voice.

"What do you mean?" I asked. Maybe it was nothing.

"I fell asleep," she said in a small voice, "and he touched me down there."

My head spun in a dizzying spiral. I felt like Alice falling down her rabbit hole.

"What happened?"

"I woke up and jumped out of bed. I was scared." Her words were tumbling out now." I yelled at him, 'What are you doing, Grandpa?' I ran across the room. I was real scared, Mommy!"

She paused for a minute to catch her breath and then went on, "He looked at me, but his eyes were different. He looked like a monster. He said, 'This is our secret, don't you dare tell your mother. Don't tell anyone!' Then his eyes got real mean."

In the silence I could hear the hammering of my heart.

Julie continued, "But, Mommy, I had to tell. You always said to tell. You said that no one is supposed to touch my privates until I'm grown up."

I drew my daughter close against me. "You poor baby. I'm never going to let him near you again. What he did was bad." I could hear the rage in my voice. "I promise I won't ever let him do that again. You were right to tell me."

I had many sleepless nights after that. I would keep my daughter safe from him no matter what. Somewhere deep in my heart I knew this was not the best answer, but what could I do? I could challenge him, but I knew that he would call Julie a liar. And then how would he behave?

"Sorry sisters end up six feet under. Betrayers are executed. People who talk have accidents. I will allow myself anything dogs do..." I could hear his threats in my ear. What would he do to Julie?

Still, I dared not tell anyone. If I told Ken that Julie had been molested, what then? Ken might do something drastic and end up in jail. I was tormented, but did nothing. Fear held me locked in its grasp. Paralyzed. But my inner voice would not stop.

Donna, face what you are dealing with...take a good look and face it.

Part III
Turning Points

Though I sometimes had to make a concerted effort to push   unpleasantness out of my mind, there were extraordinarily good things happening in life all the time.

We were such respected, public-spirited people that Ken was elected mayor of San Juan Capistrano and re-elected to a second and even a third term, a feat unequaled in the history of the community. I had framed   his campaign posters and hung them in the family gallery in the hall, and it   never ceased to warm my heart to see his picture there, earnest, honest, and so very handsome.

I had been Ken's campaign manager and busied myself running precincts, directing volunteers and making up flyers. Ken was a very popular politician, truly a man of the people who fought for senior's rights to continue to live in affordable housing, for the poor to keep their social services office, for the preservation of open space and the development of parks and baseball fields for the generations of children to come. He'd   never shrunk from a battle on behalf of those who sought his aid, and I was very proud of him; of our whole family.

Some people in the community referred to me as the "First Lady of San Juan," and that was fun. I thoroughly enjoyed attending openings of shows, cutting ribbons and sitting at the head table for so many lovely functions: Mayor and wife. The local newspapers constantly carried stories about us – our trips, our awards, our children's school activities.

We had succeeded on building something far
better than we had dared to hope. Laughter filled our
home and our hearts, and we marveled at how far we
had come from the broken homes of both our
childhoods.

If a shadow fell occasionally, I had only to look
at the happy faces in our family gallery in the upstairs
hall and the balance would tilt back. Back to the status
quo. I didn't want anything ever to disturb the life we
had forged for ourselves and our children.

Dad called me on an almost daily basis to catch
up and check up, and for the most part his interest in
our lives made me feel warm and loved.   Since
we had put more miles between us, the relationship
seemed friendlier than before, and I wasn't afraid that
he would harm Julie. All of that was behind us now. I
had managed to put it out of my mind.

But I was to learn that the past has a way of
intruding on the present, whether we want it to or not.

June 26, 1985
San Juan Capistrano, California

Danny's 14th birthday party was that night and he'd asked for *Chicken Tortilla Ole!* He always asked for it, and I was especially pleased to make it for him. School was out for the summer and with great enjoyment, I was throwing myself full-throttle into the joys of motherhood.

I was deboning the chicken with the help of my housekeeper, Rosa, when I saw a new Camaro pulling into the driveway.

Who could that be? Between the telephone calls and the interruptions, I was having a difficult time getting my casserole layered. My irritation gave way to surprise when I recognized Cee Cee behind the wheel. Her baby daughter, Keely, was with her.

"Cee Cee!" I yelled enthusiastically as I rushed out to the driveway. I hugged her and glanced down at her beautiful dark-haired baby. "I haven't seen you in ages. How do you happen to be here?"

"Oh, Donna, I should have called. Rand had a toothache. Sandy took him on an emergency appointment." We were all very proud of Sandy and grateful to have a dentist in the family. She took care of all the family's teeth.

"I have to go and get him in an hour. I just wanted to see you, wanted you to see how big Keely's getting." Cee Cee spoke sincerely, huge blue eyes looking to mine for approval. A kind of sadness emanated from her pretty face.

"Well goodness, I am so glad you did! My heavens, Keely is getting huge and soooo cute! Is she eight months now?"

A short time later, lemonade in one hand and adorable Keely posed on the opposite hip, Cee Cee leaned against the tiled counter in my kitchen. I went back to deboning while Cee Cee caught me up on all the latest family news from Los Angeles.

Her husband Rand's musical career was taking off and he was frequently on European or Japanese tours with his heavy metal group. His latest album was a big hit in Japan and he was soon to open at Madison Square Garden. She had every reason to be happy, but it soon became clear that she was not doing very well emotionally. She had been feeling suicidal more and more often, but she knew better with a new baby and four others to care for.

Listening to her, I realized that Cee Cee had always had trouble with depression. Even before she got pregnant at 17 with her oldest daughter, Anne, she was either incredibly happy or miserably sad. As I aligned my corn tortillas and filled them with chicken, I knew that today was all about sad.

"Donna," her voice filled with misery. "I really am at the end of my rope. Daddy won't leave me alone. He drives me crazy. When Rand and I are on tour he follows us. Last month in Nashville, Dad showed up at our hotel right when we were making love. We were 2,000 miles away and there he was at our door, unannounced and uninvited!" Her passion flamed. "He actually came into our room, lay on the bed and asked me to fetch him a soft drink over cracked ice. "

"Rand has about had it with me. He's furious and wants Daddy away from us. When Dad comes around every day, Rand leaves the house."

Her voice was stronger now, charged with anger. "You know that's why Henri left me, because of Dad. He said he was always in our faces."

"Cee Cee, as long as he's supporting you, he's going to think he has a right to barge in any time he wants. We don't live all the way down here by accident. Ken was not about to spend a lifetime with Dad."

"Don't just hint, Cee Cee," I added firmly. "Dad doesn't hear hints. He'll even call down here at weird times like after 11 o'clock at night. He knows that I go to sleep early. Ken's short with him and never wakes me up. That's how you have to handle Dad. He's like a big lonesome baby. Mostly, he likes to read his novels to me," I concluded with a shrug.

"It's worse than that." Cee Cee's voice dropped an octave or two. There was a long pause. Her lids covered her eyes. I was adding green chilies to my casserole layers.

"Anne told me he has bothered her." My heart stopped at the mention of my 17-year-old niece. Suddenly I was at attention. I could feel my face turning red. What I had dreaded all these years, what I had never allowed myself to think...

"What do you mean, bothered her? " I asked cautiously in as controlled a voice as I could muster.

A long pause followed. "He forces himself on her."

"What do you mean?" I couldn't keep the urgency from my voice.

"He forces himself on her!"

"What are you telling me?" I had to know exactly what she meant.

"He makes her have sex! She hates him. Wants to kill him. He hurts her. She's so tiny. God, Donna I don't know what to do. I can't get him to stop. He bothers me, too." She sounded like she was choking.

I cleaned my hand and shakily led Cee Cee and Keely, still in her arms, to the sofa. "Tell me about it, sweetheart," I forced myself to calm down. I had never solved a problem by panicking. I would not panic now, though adrenaline-fueled pounding was loud in my ears.

Forty-five excruciating minutes later, Cee Cee and Keely left to collect Rand and return to Los Angeles. I was stunned.

All those warm birthday thoughts I had been filled with an hour before had vanished. I was dazed from the ghastly tale Cee Cee had so haltingly revealed. Not only had our father molested her when she was very young, but by the time she was eight-years-old he had forced intercourse on her. It was horrible.

She had gone on to tell me that he had done the same to her daughter, Anne. Anne had finally told Cee Cee what had been going on all these years. Cee Cee kept Anne safe from him now by sacrificing herself.

This had been very difficult to hear. I could not imagine that Cee Cee at 35 years-of-age was still under Dad's control. The bile lodged in my throat.

I learned that Daddy had given Cee Cee over to our grandfather, Big Ray, who also had molested her. I was devastated. Those whispers in my mind the day we poured through old boxes turned into shouts. Big Ray, too! But I had loved my grandfather. I wanted desperately to hold his memory sacred.

Cee Cee also suspected that our youngest sister, 15-year-old Diedre, might have been molested by Dad, too. Diedre had lived with Bernie, her mother, since Dad divorced her back in the early 70s. Dad saw little of Diedre these days. Cee Cee thought she was probably safe now.

I quickly calculated the present risk. Everyone was away from Dad except Cee Cee. All the younger girls – Diedre, Connie, Annie and Julie – were away from him, and Keely was just an eight-month-old baby. Cee Cee was clearly the only one left in danger now. I admonished her to find a new job like the one she had held for years as Hollywood booking agent. She needed to be independent from Dad. She had to get away from him.

Cee Cee was frightened and told me she considered telling her husband. After a long while she concluded, "No he'd leave me if he knew!" She started crying again after that.

Cee Cee was forced to drop out of high school when she had become pregnant with Anne. She had then attended a special school for unwed pregnant girls. While there Cee Cee performed with such superiority that she was chosen as the class valedictorian. Dad must have been the most surprised. He'd always told us she was stupid.

I remember watching her from my seat in the auditorium during her graduation ceremony. She was very pregnant and very young, but her valedictory speech was eloquent and well-delivered. I was very proud of my sister that day.

Today's news from her had raised the tiny hairs on my arms and sucked my breath away. This was beyond my wildest nightmares. I had used the word "crazy" to describe Dad's bizarre actions, but I knew that he was not crazy. Crazy was not knowing right from wrong.

Dad certainly knew right from wrong. He had a sophisticated high-tech job, was educated, and wrote novels, studied. He'd even been president of his yacht club. Knowing that Dad didn't qualify as actually crazy was perhaps the most frightening thought of all.

Cee Cee also told me about Connie. She was part of my father's second family with Bernie. Cee Cee reported that Connie recently had come to her for help when she ran away from Dad because he continued to molest her. *Oh no, not Connie too!*

What about Sandy? I remembered her agony when she revealed to me a few years earlier that Dad had sexually abused her. When Sandy reported him to Child Protective Services, the agency had simply done a cursory investigation. Because no child was living with him, there was no case. As always, our dad remained unaffected.

After that Dad took every opportunity to complain that Sandy was treacherous. "One who is treacherous might be eliminated," He intoned solemnly, sending chills down my spine.

I sat back and tried to think. The pain burned into my soul. I had promised myself that my nightmare was behind me, that everything was okay. Nothing bad could happen like it had when I was little. And here it was, spilled out all over my beautiful home where I had felt safe from that agony. Until now.

June 27, 1985
At Home
San Juan Capistrano

I awoke with Cee Cee's words whirling in my head and felt compelled to go on examining my memories. Something else was trying to force its way into my consciousness. I leafed through my imaginary Rolodex and came to "T" for my brother Trey. He was just a bit older than my own son Rick. Trey had just turned 21, loved school and college life. He was a dependable, sincere young man.

I recalled Dad's voice, syrupy on the surface, contradicting the sly underhanded messages it held.

"Trey's a bonehead. He'll never amount to anything."

"Cee Cee was dropped on her head as a baby. She'll always be a mess."

I realized that Dad consistently said terrible things to me about each of my siblings: my brothers, Trey and Chad, and my sisters, Sandy, Cee Cee, Diedre and Connie. He was playing us one against the other. I'd often heard him refer to Cee Cee as a "savage." Our father was apparently a cold calculating liar. He had manipulated us by dividing us with lies.

To our faces he was love and kisses; lots of smiles, extolling our virtues. His favorite line to us all was, "I love you more than anything." Behind our backs, he invented the most fiendish of lies. Because of our father, we really did not trust each other. I knew I did not trust any of my siblings with my truth. Divide and conquer was the basic warfare strategy. I recalled that my long-widowed grandmother, Maymie, once began dating a man Dad didn't approve of. My father put detectives on him and forced Maymie to stop their friendship. Dad ran the whole show, the whole family. He always had.

"The most bonded to the abusing parent." Yes. I'd once read that in a self-help book. How interesting that it did not make much of an impression on me at the time, but when I thought about it now, I realized it was true. Who did I want to be the most perfect for? Daddy, of course. The abusing parent.

How often had I hid my real feelings behind a mask of Super Happy. How about Super Agreeable? That too. Miss Cooperative, afraid to speak up. Afraid to look at the truth. Afraid to admit how horribly Daddy hurt me, too.

I had never told Cee Cee my own secrets about Dad, about what he had done to me, not even yesterday when she was pouring her heart out. What if she told Dad that she had told me? Cee Cee might well tell Dad. I did not want to even consider what those consequences might be.

June 28, 1985
San Juan Capistrano

My nights were sleepless. What should I do? I concluded that everyone was safe for now, and Cee Cee had promised to get away from Dad. Did I really want to get involved in what was happening between Dad and his second family? There was an impatient part of me that was not altogether sympathetic about Cee Cee's dependent status, but I was desperately sorry for all that had happened to her.

For years I encouraged her to go to college or work, anything to stand on her own.

I had studied Eric Berne's work on the psychological games people play and understood that Dad and Cee Cee were playing "victim-rescuer." I had shown her how Dad liked to be Big Daddy, doling out money and favors as he chose. Dad always kept Cee Cee down by repeating the story of her being dropped on her head. She was "damaged goods," he'd say.

I knew the only way to stop these games was for her to become independent, to get away from Dad. Cee Cee had remained dependent, however, always needing grocery money, advice and even one of Dad's houses to live in.

Perhaps he talked about me behind my back, too, but he always told me to my face that I was beautiful and competent. And he had never turned me over to Big Ray or anyone else. I wondered how he had decided to do that with Cee Cee, but not me. I was grateful that Big Ray had been a wonderful grandfather to me but reflected for a long time on how Dad and Big Ray perceived the difference between us. I didn't like the answer I came up with.

Cee Cee, our father's illegitimate child, was thought to be expendable. Dad must have always viewed her as worthless. Perhaps he actually believed it possible that some humans were superior to others. Yes…I strained my mind. He clearly believed that men were superior to women; hated that women had the right to vote, and resented having them on the road behind the wheel of a car. His vocabulary had always been filled with words straight out of a Victorian novel, like "mistress," "class," "bastard," "cuckold."

My mind was reaching back to things long forgotten that I must have always heard. Finally, I could hear my father's dogmatic voice: "Hitler had the right idea. Those Hebes are unfit to do business with. They deserved everything they got." "Blondes are higher class than brunettes." "Jigaboos are mentally inferior."

It was incredible. He must actually believe these ridiculous thoughts! What seemed like relatively banal red-neck talk, which I had spent a lifetime tuning out, took on new proportions. I knew that soldiers depersonalized the enemy by stereotyping, and labeling. It made the horrors of war bearable. "Gooks, Chinks, Japs, slants, slopes, sons of bitches, bastards."

Non-humans. I saw it then what Dad must think: Cee Cee, a bastard, worthless, her feelings could not matter. Anne, like Cee Cee as inferior, expendable… Beautiful, talented, clever, loving Cee Cee. Funny Cee Cee, always ready with a joke.

And what about our grandmother who said that she had been sold? This was too horrible. I wanted to switch the channel in my head, but it wouldn't switch.

Big Ray and Maymie? I had known it once, for a while, years ago. Suddenly, it all became clear again. Poor Maymie. I understood. She had just been a little kid.

I paused for a moment and thought of my always-youthful, energetic grandmother. She was educated, cultivated, a lady. Through her hard work she had pulled the family back from the devastation of the Depression. She had found happiness in her life, dancing, enjoying all of us, reading, visiting with her many friends. She, who had made so much of her life, had gone through the humiliation of being sold. It must have felt like a life sentence.

Why had Big Ray never bothered me? Perhaps he attributed some special quality to me. I had always felt something like that. I was born within wedlock, which seemed a rather select status in our family. Was that it? They abused little Cee Cee because she was born out of wedlock? I could not fathom what life must have been like, was like now. It all seemed more depraved than the horror stories by V.C. Andrews my children read, *Flowers in the Attic.* That had been revolting. Freddie terrorizing Elm Street. But all those stories had been *fiction.* What does one do when faced with the undeniable fact that she is living in the middle of something worse than fiction?

Not having an answer to that question, I switched back to Cee Cee's childhood. Mine certainly had not been ideal, but still I had my father's last name, my father slept at our house. I did not feel like Cinderella to two legitimate sisters. How must it have been for her always to call her father, "Ray-Ray" and to lie about Sandy and me? Clearly the implication had to have been that she was not "good enough" to be a real sister or daughter.

June 29, 1985
San Juan Capistrano

Still feeling anxious after several days, I called Cee Cee to see how she was. Her mood had greatly improved. She was much better since our talk. She reported that sharing it had taken some of the shame and fear out of it.

Cee Cee believed that everyone was safe. She would just make Dad stop, make him leave her alone. It would be okay. She reassured me again that Anne was clear of Dad now. She decided to quit answering the phone every time he called, and to stop going to his house all the time to clean for him.

I felt relief. By the end of the second week after Cee Cee's visit, I was able to push my fears back behind their special safety-locked door, behind the tumblers and steel. Pushing my fears away seemed to be getting more and more difficult, but the pain and the fury had to be buried.

If Dad knew that anyone had told on him, it could be deadly. I kept placating myself by remembering that everyone was safe now. There was nothing more I could do.

I knew I would not consider telling Ken. He might do something drastic. I also had three children to consider and our respect in the community. Ken was now in his third term as mayor. I forced my attentions back to my family and our summer plans. I had to put this to rest.

And Dad, had he changed? I didn't know what to think. This was all so difficult for me. After everything, I still loved my dad...

August 5, 1985
Avalon Bay
Catalina Island

I cleared away the breakfast utensils and went out on the deck of our boat. The bright sun danced off the water. It promised to be a golden day.

Hoping to cool off, I dove into the crystal water and swam into the fairway in front of our boat. As I hung from one hand, grasping the mooring line, I could see that someone was aboard my father's similar boat moored a short distance away. I had not seen him since Cee Cee's explosive news five weeks before. I was now finally sleeping again at night. Things also seemed to be going okay for Cee Cee.

I took a deep breath, let go of the mooring line and swam towards Dad's boat. He was sitting reading in the aft area.

"Hi, Dad,"

"Hi, Bugger. How are you, Honey?" His voice was filled with joy at discovering me in the water below.

"Super. It's a real challenge cooking on the boat's alcohol stove."

"Come aboard. I'm just working on this new mystery novel that takes place here in Avalon. Can I read to you for a while?" he asked.

"Sure, let me climb up and dry out for a bit."

I dried my hair with a towel I found on the deck, then pulled a white plastic chair around and sat down. "Okay, Dad. Read on." The warm sun soaked into my wet skin. I closed my eyes as Dad read.

This story was an action murder mystery with some Hollywood bad guys behind a Catalina death plot. He called it *Escape From Evil*. As he read on for several minutes, I became interested. It was about a high-roller type who owned a 70-foot yacht moored in Avalon Harbor. As the story continued the murderer nonchalantly ordered one of his burly employees to find an eight-year-old girl and bring her back to the yacht for sexual acts.

My eyes snapped open. Dad was reading this horrible story to me with a straight face and in a calm voice. I was seeing the perverted story come alive in my minds' eyes. I was that little girl.

"I can't hear anymore..." Tears sprang to my eyes as I turned away from him.

"What's wrong?" Dad asked in his most innocent, puzzled voice.

"I can't do this." My voice cracked as I muttered, "I'm not okay about what you did to me when I was little."

He looked at me blankly, making a note with his pencil in the margin of his notebook.

I rushed on. "Last semester a girl in my speech class gave a speech on incest and I got panicky and started to hyperventilate. I was afraid I might faint. I'm not okay with what you did to me when I was little! Ever. I'm not okay."

I turned my face away, my chin quivering. I was struggling for control. I had not confronted my father in years. We had always pretended that it had never happened. A long silence followed.

"I'm sorry," I heard him mumble.

"I'd better not hear any more of these novels," I warned. "This upsets me too much." I spoke in strangled words, careful not to reveal any more, certainly nothing of what Cee Cee had so recently told me. I might jeopardize both of our lives.

At that moment my half-sister, Connie, who had been below in the cabin, came out. "Hi, Donna, nice day!" She greeted me warmly.

"Yes...ah....er....I've got to go!"

My father's attention had turned back to his writing. He didn't have anything to say to me as I left. He seemed totally unaffected by what I had said. I climbed down the swim step, eased myself into the cold water and swam back to our boat. My father was still writing notes in his book.

A nugget of truth nudged me as I kicked through the chilly waters: "No conscience." I had read that someone without a conscience couldn't really ever get one. Sociopaths didn't have a conscience. They felt no remorse or guilt. They could only veil their disorder to blend in with society. It was only upon close inspection that they could be detected.

The quiet inner voice spoke to me, *Donna, your father is not the good guy you've always pretended him to be.* That gentle inner voice would not go away. It kept haunting me.

I remembered other interactions when his response to me had been peculiar. The year before he found a 21-year-old waitress in a restaurant he frequented for breakfast. He had given her a 2½ carat diamond ring, trying to get her to marry him.

That morning I was showing my paintings at a local outdoor exhibit and he made a date to visit me there. He would bring his new lady to meet me. I was proud of a painting I had just completed of myself at age one. It was the centerpiece of my exhibit. I knew Daddy would adore it.

I waited for him all day, but he never showed up. I was about to drive out of the parking lot when I saw Dad waving and honking. I stopped and got out of the car.

"Hi Donnie!" He sounded youthful and happy. "Wow, I'm glad I caught you. I want you to meet Kitty!"

Introductions were made, the diamond was shown. I tried to force the ice from my voice. "Nice to meet you, Kitty. Nice ring!"

"Donnie, she wants to have a whole bunch of kids the same as I do!" He was breathless with excitement. I felt like his mother. He had his new fiancée and dazzling plans. I stood feeling dull with my little handpainted plates packed into my car. I swallowed my hurt, trying to ignore the fact that Kitty was younger than my son, Dad's grandson! Caught up in their own music, they did not notice my weak performance.

I went with them for a quick dinner. Dad as usual hit me up to pay for it. "She's bucks up." He said to Kitty. I guess he missed the irony of buying her a huge ring to her with his money and then conning his daughter into paying for dinner. Afterward, at the car, I tried again to get the attention I had hoped for with my new painting. I handed it to Dad, holding my breath, anxious for the praise I knew would be forthcoming. I felt proud. My heart gave an extra little thump. I knew this self-portrait would really thrill him.

He glanced down briefly at the painting. "That's nice, Honey. So what do you think of Kitty? Isn't she something?" He beamed as he pulled her into another hug.

I stood alone. That had not been the time to examine this idea closely, but now, as I swam away to the safety of my boat, that small thought gnawed at me. Sociopath.

November 1988
At School

Sitting at my large desk in my corner office at the college where I had been teaching for twenty-two years, I paused and looked up at the wall in front of my desk. It danced with pictures of my family. My three children smiled at me from dozens of photos taken over the years. They were precious to me. My office was also my sanctuary.

My students were eager to catch a glimpse into my private life. They often brought their friends and other students to see my picture wall.

Since Cee Cee's ugly revelation a few years earlier, I devoted my energies even more to my family, my portrait painting, and my students. They all comforted me. I knew how to keep busy, how to keep control

Today something special had happened in my classroom. Something that reflected why teaching was so important to me. As my students were filing out after class, I had an opportunity to say something to a young man whom I'd also had in another class. I'd been noticing a tremendous change in him lately.

He was lagging behind zipping up his backpack. It hung heavily under its great weight of textbooks. As Tran ambled past my podium, I spoke to him.

"So, Tran," I used my most casual voice, "it seems I'm noticing a change in you lately. Am I?" I smiled warmly. He had been a tough one to get through to.

He looked directly at me, his dark almond-shaped eyes as deeply serious as always. "I found out from you that I was not a freak."

I laughed. "Who would ever say that about you?"

"I always knew I was freak," his tone was matter-of-fact. "I've never had many friends. I haven't really fit in. Sports were out. I'm too small."

"Tran, I never thought of you as different."

"Well, I thought so until you taught us about those personality types. I have always hated everything about myself." He paused and looked self-consciously at me. "I'm okay with me now."

"Well, I'm glad." I smiled at him.

He nodded his delicately featured head and moved toward the door. I knew that our conversation was over. Not many words were exchanged but what had transpired was remarkable.

I had met Tran, a skinny 16-year-old, the year before when he had been an advanced placement high school student taking my college public speaking class. He never mixed in with the other students. He was aloof and unfriendly, seeming to be disdainful of me and the subject, superior to us all. He was going to be a scientist. His attitude was not an asset. He earned a B in my class, probably the first in his life.

Then at the first of the next semester, there he was coming in to register late for another one of my classes. I was shocked to see him. For weeks he seldom spoke to anyone. Then suddenly after a lesson on Sheldon's personality types, he began to change. I think he discovered that he was not alone. He was not only normal, but he had been described in a scientific textbook.

I felt Tran's pain for a moment. Our culture stresses the active, outdoorsy type, so that those who are less athletic often feel inadequate. It made me angry. Why wasn't it okay to be who you are? Why can't we be all colors, all sizes, all cultures, all religions? Why can't we just be people who are happy and sad, who feel pain and joy?

Students like Tran who acknowledged that I made a difference in their lives came along more often than not in my teaching career and made it all worthwhile for me. I knew that my gift was an ability to connect with my students, helping them to see just how important they were. School was such a wonderfully safe place for me.

July 15, 1989
San Juan Capistrano

Having the summer off from teaching had its positive and negative sides. I enjoyed the freedom to do as I chose, but when I had too much spare time, I found myself worrying. Sometimes I worried about the uncontrollable flashes of the past, other times I brooded about Keely. I needed to distract myself, so I planned a big picnic celebration for Julie's 21st birthday.

While I was working at my desk, making a list of supplies for the party, the telephone rang. I reached for the phone.

"Donnie?" asked the youthful voice I immediately recognized as my father's.

"Hi, Dad! How's your fancy new hip today?" I asked with a smile, successfully stuffing my anxieties for the moment.

"Hey, a few more of these operations and I'll be bionic man! It's amazing. I can actually walk now. No more crippled old fogy."

"That's great, Dad. The physical therapist has been a big help, hasn't she?"

"Yeah, but my speed isn't 20 steps and a pat on the back. Fogy baloney. I'm ready to think about body surfing."

"Dad, is it better being back at the beach? I can't believe you ever moved away from the water."

"So much better. It's too hot in Hollywood. Hey, I called to tell you that I received the invitation to Julie's party today. Twenty-one. Where does the time go?"

"I don't know."

"Donna, that invitation is just too much. It's so clever I can't believe it."

"Do you really think so?"

"Really! How many girls have a painting of themselves at age one printed in color on an engraved invitation? Especially one painted by their own mother! It's beyond clever. Your talent is bursting at the seams!"

His words made me feel special and loved. I still reveled in Dad's praise.

"I know I'm biting off an awfully lot to try to barbeque for 130 guests."

"Ah, people pitch in. And, Honey, we don't all have to eat at once. Some will still be swimming, some playing volleyball, besides it's going to be the best party this family has ever had."

"Oh, Dad, do you think so?"

"Angel, it can't miss. It'll have everything. You're the hostess. Oh, Donnie, someone's at the door. Gotta go. I wanted to tell you all about taking Keely to the baby store. I got her three new dresses. She modeled each one like Miss America. So cute. I want to tell you all about it. Gotta get off now. I'll call back later."

"Okay, I want to hear about those dresses. Miss America, huh? Keely is something else."

"The party will be perfect. No more worrying. Kisses."

"Bye, Dad."

As I hung up the telephone, I turned my attention immediately back to the table decorations and centerpieces. Balloons. We would need balloons.

August 10, 1989
San Juan Capistrano

This morning while I fed Cory and Cassie, my two dogs, one of those horrible pictures flashed in my mind. I fought it as hard as I could, but lately feeding the dogs was becoming an increasingly powerful trigger to my memory. For some reason the same image came into my mind almost every day.

I would see Daddy climbing off of me in the dark, when I was little, in the trailer on a trip to Chicago. I was pretending to be asleep in my sleeping bag on the floor. I could make out Dad's shape in the shadows of that trailer. He was going over to my small sleeping sister. Maymie was asleep in the front bed. My sweet little Sandy was in the double bed in the back.

Oh no...stop. Ugly, sick pictures. Images that I had never permitted myself to see. I wondered just how much more of this I could take.

They were coming all the time now. Sometimes different ones. They always left me trembling, nauseous, and frightened. The most alarming part was that I could not control them. Donna, the master of personal control, now could not stop the foul images reeling across her mind.

I realized that these episodes had been occurring for several years. They had become more and more frequent since 1985 when Cee Cee visited me. I knew that I was deliberately trying to hide from their meaning, from the truth. But my mind would no longer allow it.

That gentle voice, the loving spirit who comforted me from within, was no longer reassuring me. I thought of my afternoon rests and the moments before I fell asleep at night. I could hear the gentle voice pushing me, urging me.

Donna, what about Keely? She is four-years-old now. She is almost school age. The age you were when you can remember him touching you. What about Keely? You must protect the children...

My concern had intensified since January when a big group of us had met at our boat. That was the first time I had really spent time with Keely.

We had immediately hit it off. She spent the entire day in my lap as we toured San Pedro Harbor in the January chill. We had cuddled and laughed. I photographed our hands together; my strong tanned one with her tiny, pale one lying inside my palm.

An idea for an interesting painting came to me and I took many pictures. I had painted her amazing face when she was two, and the portrait had been published in an artist's magazine. Keely was precious; her lips were a bright natural red like her father's and her eyes were iridescent blue, fringed with a thick row of dark lashes. She was a very pretty child.

By the end of the day, straddling my lap and looking directly at me, playing absently with the rings on my finger, she said, "Aunt Donna, I'm so glad you fell in love with me!"

I had fallen in love with her. Her observation knocked me for a loop; she was so bright and direct. I laughed at her child's honesty and hugged her to me. We both wrapped up in my jacket against the wind of the brisk day. My heart spilled over with love for this four-year-old.

That day was the start of a heavy correspondence. My refrigerator was now covered with her drawings. I was getting more and more involved in Keely's life. She even had her mother call me once a week. We had wonderful talks about her pets, her nursery school, and her baby brother, Kyle.

A few months later, I dropped in unexpectedly to visit Cee Cee and her family. Cee Cee and Rand were going out for the evening. Cee Cee was on the telephone trying to arrange for Connie to babysit. Connie couldn't, but she said Dad would. He said he wanted to take Keely to see a new movie.

Overhearing this conversation, panic seized me. I butted in, almost hissing at Cee Cee.

"No! Don't let Keely go with him, anywhere, alone, *ever!*"

My vehemence startled her. It startled me. I didn't know where it came from, but I was alarmed. After a long moment, understanding splashed across Cee Cee's face. She turned back to the telephone.

"Ah, Connie, that's okay. I'll make other arrangements for Keely. Thanks. I'll talk to you soon."

When she hung up the phone I admonished her to *never* let him babysit. Finally, after my urgent lecture, she had shaken her head in mute agreement. We both knew that Dad had been very ill. He had almost died from his recent prostate problems. I tried to tell myself that he was an invalid. He was too old to be a threat. Cee Cee probably told herself the same things, but I was not really reassured. I lived so far away I knew that I was powerless to protect Keely. Or was I?

When I got home, I took the dogs for a long walk. As they bounded along, I thought of Ken. He was the one who insisted that we seek this rural life, introducing his beach girl to horses, orange groves, cowboys and swallows. He was such a steadying influence on my life. What would I ever do without him? It was a chilling thought.

It took me a minute to realize why I was contemplating the consequences of losing Ken, and when I did, it made me even more afraid.

August 18, 1989
San Juan Capistrano

"Donnie?"

"Oh, hi Dad." I answered distractedly, hearing the familiar voice of my father across the telephone line. My flashbacks were getting worse, and it was becoming more and more difficult to make small talk with him, as the mechanism that used to guard my memories gradually broke down.

"Honey, I called to say hi. I'm still thinking about Julie's party. It was fantastic."

"I'm glad you enjoyed it," I responded quietly.

"You should see the tent city that Keely and Russ are making across the chairs in my living room. They're having great fun."

We talked on for a short while. As I hung up the phone, the lump in my stomach reminded me how anxious I was feeling about Keely, and about the pictures from my memory that flashed so frequently now. I could visualize precious little Keely in my father's living room. How could Cee Cee let him babysit her children? The worry was eating away at me.

Safely alone in the late afternoon seclusion of my silent home, desperate for some shred of reassurance about Keely, I went into Julie's empty bedroom. It was just the way she'd left it three years ago when she went away to college. I opened her double closet doors and sat on the floor in front of the bookcase. I was searching for her textbook on abnormal psychology.

I located it quickly and turned to the index where I immediately found an entry for sexual deviates. I turned to the page and began reading, hoping to discover some information to calm my fears about Keely's safety. I knew so little, truly, almost nothing about this subject. I had always been afraid to read even the bare essential information about child molestation, incest or father-daughter rape. Just the mention of the topic sent me into a panic attack.

I knew this book would be helpful. I scanned the chapters: Incest, Pedophiles, Rape. "Pedophiles start with their eldest child and continue. They continue to abuse into their seventies. They never stop." Those words loomed out of the textbook at me: *"They never stop!"*

Just last night Dad had called me and put Keely on the telephone. Her baby voice said, "Aunt Donna, I am so lucky you love me."

And then my father had come back on. Wistfully he had said, "Keely told me yesterday that I am the nicest man she knows and that she wants to marry me. I told her that they won't let us. Donnie, she is the only woman who loves me."

His remark shook me to my foundations. The hidden recesses of my soul began to open, releasing more pictures from my memory. What I saw did not reassure me about Keely's safety. *Woman who loves me...........woman who loves me........... oh, my god! She is practically a baby. She is not a woman!*

August 23, 1989
San Juan Capistrano

I spent an hour in the mall looking for a birthday gift for Ken's mother. I wanted another little gift to add to the chalk drawing I had done of her cat. We were having a dinner party for her that night.

I was browsing at B. Dalton Bookseller when a display of the book *Toxic Parents* by Dr. Susan Forward caught my eye. Interesting title. I purchased a copy. A few days later I began reading it.

> There are many types of physical abusers. Many of these people look, talk and act just like human beings, but they are monsters totally devoid of the feeling and characteristics that give most of us our humanity...these people defy comprehension. There is no logic to their behavior.

As I read on, a tight feeling filled me. It was as if I were reading about my own life.

> Many physically abusive parents enter adulthood with tremendous emotional deficits and unmet needs. Emotionally, they are children. They often look upon their own children as surrogate parents to fulfill the emotional needs that their real parents never fulfilled. The abuser becomes enraged when his child can't [won't] meet his needs.

I could hardly believe what I was reading. Daddy had turned me into his little mother by the time I was two. My childhood was filled with preparing his baths, his meals, massaging his back and keeping his house. To deny his demands, any of his demands, was to meet a violent rage. I thought about my wrist being bent backwards. I thought about the late night violence.

> He [the abuser] lashes out, and at the moment, the child is more of a surrogate parent than ever because it is the abuser's parent at whom the abuser is truly enraged.

It did not take much speculation to conjure up an image of Dad as a little boy, furiously staying on the back fence when his mother arrived home after a trip she took around the world. Dad had told us of that trip hundreds of times, and even when he was in his 50s and 60s he sounded like a petulant child.

"She was gone for more than a year," he'd complained. "I never called her "mother" after that."

He never forgave Maymie for leaving him.

I read about the role reversal of the abused child with the passive "other" parent. The child assumes responsibility for the protection of that parent as if she was the child.

> By allowing herself [himself] to be overwhelmed by helplessness, the inactive parent can more easily deny her silent complicity in the abuse. And by becoming protective, or by rationalizing the silent partner's inactivity, the abused child can more easily deny the fact that both parents have failed her [him].

I thought about my mother's role in my life. She had always excused our hardships by saying, "we were just surviving." She clearly saw herself as a victim, not as an adult protector of her own children. In the past ten years, my mother had questioned me about Dad on several occasions.

"Your father never touched you girls, did he?"

Her head would be shaking no when she asked the question. It was easy to answer her. I gave her the answer she wanted.

"No, Mom."

I felt obligated to protect her. I did not want to believe that my mother had failed me too. I wanted to believe that she loved me.

I was dazed by the section of the book entitled "The Keeper of the Family Secret." It could have been written about me. I knew that I would never have bought this book if I had known what it was really about.

> Moments of tenderness, love and support keep [a victim] yearning for a normal relationship with him [her father]. As a part of that bonding she believes she has to keep secret the truth about her father's behavior. A "good girl" would never betray her family.

What was I going to do about this? What was I going to do about Keely and Daddy? I knew that the anxious feelings I had been experiencing on and off all summer were about my fear for Keely's safety. She was fast approaching a dangerous age. She was now four. Five and six loomed perilously close.

Cee Cee guaranteed me that Keely was never alone with him, that her older brothers Russ, 9, and Jess, 14, were always present. I knew Dad's modus operandi. The boys were no protection at all from grandpa, the babysitter. The more I read, the more convinced I became that Keely was in serious danger of being abused.

My logical mind returned to his hip replacement surgery in May. He used a walker. Dad also had severe kidney damage, and ketones in his blood from his prostate problem the year before. He had been very sick. He was almost bedridden. Was I just over-reacting? I read on in the book:

> If one were a victim of childhood sexual
> abuse, he or she could not cure themselves.
> Such victims require professional help.

I thought of my frequent flashbacks and I knew that I had to do something. I knew that my mind was not going to let me evade the issue this time. I decided to make an appointment with a therapist. I told Ken and my family that I was planning on getting my professional counseling certification, and I wanted to get the therapy requirement out of the way first.

Ken knew that I was about to enroll in a doctoral program and agreed that I should do whatever would work best for me.

My gentle inner voice kept prodding me. *Is Keely safe? Is she?*

August 30, 1989
Rose's Office
Newport Beach, California

One week later, Sandy accompanied me on my first visit with the therapist, Rose, a nice plump woman in her mid-fifties. Sandy stayed a short while, and then left us alone in the pale pinkness of Rose's silent office. Rose looked at me and quietly said, "So tell me what has brought you here?"

A long moment passed. Finally, chin quivering, I blurted out the words which I had so long held back: "When I was a little girl, my father molested me."

Tears came. They overwhelmed me. I was terrified; for I had violated every rule I had been taught. I had betrayed Daddy to a stranger. I had told the secret! Somehow I forged ahead and began to tell her everything. I knew I had to gain control of my flashbacks, the turmoil in my mind.

This was my first step.

September 10, 1989
San Juan Capistrano

I hung up the telephone. I'd been chatting with Dad. Dread tore at me, terrifying me.

Dad was going to babysit with Keely overnight.

Armed with my new knowledge, I had become hyper-vigilant. Dad's every word in every conversation took on new meaning. I'd made some pathetic inquires about Keely and the logistics of the babysitting. I was still desperately hoping to extinguish my growing suspicions.

"Donnie," Dad had begun, "Cee Cee and Rand wore their black leather rocker clothes today. Rand was in stage makeup. They told me that a pedestrian was so frightened by their appearance that he crossed the street to avoid walking near them."

"Dad," I said, "I'm worried about Keely." He thought that I was reacting to his story. I meant that I was worried about Keely's spending the night with him.

Dad always played the innocent. I knew there was nothing to be gained by confronting him about Keely's spending the night at his house. But my mind just would not let go of the thought of Keely. She was so tiny and so trusting. She was just a little girl who loved her Grandpa.

Donna, do something before it's too late! You have to protect Keely.

I could not pretend to be okay when I was frantic with worry. It was becoming harder for me to make telephone small talk with Dad. A week or so later, I could not deal with him at all. Ken made excuses for me for a few weeks, but I knew that I could only be "showing apartments" so many times.

I told my husband that I was dealing with some childhood issues in therapy and was too upset just now to talk to my father. Ken accepted this, but it was awkward for him to keep making excuses for me. He didn't really understand why I wouldn't speak with Dad.

By September 15th, I knew I could not keep dodging Dad's calls. I wrote a letter to explain my sudden change in behavior, hoping that it would forestall the daily calls and buy me some time. I claimed grief over Danny's moving away to college and the recent death of my horse, Windy. I was too afraid to rock the boat by telling the truth.

I dreaded opening the envelope that promptly came back in my father's exact engineer's lettering. Ken was sitting next to me in my dressing room while I read the eight page letter. When I finished it, I passed it wordlessly to him.

"My word, look at his condescending tone," Ken laughed.

"Kenny, this is not about what you think. This is about something else I cannot tell you," I said. I knew that I had not succeeded in slipping past Dad's watchful eye. He was not accepting the written explanation I had sent. By not taking his calls, I had started something frightening.

The entire tone of his letter was sarcastic. He started by calling me his "Little Pen Pal." He gave chatty information about all the family members, subtly reminding me of what I was cutting myself off from. He patronized me with advice about how to live my life, suggesting that I had my values and priorities all wrong and that I was a workaholic. His tone of superiority and his threats told me without a doubt that I was embarking on war.

He included a strange poem he had written within the letter:

The troops, nearly always innocent of the nature of war, march boldly forth to the beat of the drum.

Other innocents, at home, sit on volcanic soil never aware of its true nature.

The leaders of both rarely apprise them of the fact.

All go merrily to their various fates.

I was deeply frightened by the letter and not quite clear about the poem. I knew it was some kind of threat for the tremendous act of defiance I was committing by not talking to him on the phone. I considered calling and smoothing things over before the war got out of hand.

I thought of Keely's little hand in mine, secure, trusting. I heard, "Aunt Donna, I am so lucky to have you love me." My inner voice kept nagging me about her safety. I felt that my reputation as a human being was on the line. I was a mother, a school teacher, a decent citizen. I must keep Keely safe.

I knew that I had indeed started something I could not stop. An angry part of me goaded me on to respond to my father's letter. I would use his same sarcastic tone. Inwardly I composed the words I would never send:

Dear Dad,

I got a kick out of the closing of your letter as you described sitting back and watching, "One Man's Family." I agree our family is fascinating. What a brilliant plot.

One handsome, charming man molests babies, then rapes them, starting at about age 8, and continues the sexual abuse until they can escape. Then the father watches how they handle their own personal devastation.

The first child, Donna, the compliant one, tried to pretend it never happened. She tried to be perfect to cover for her own overwhelming sense of shame.

Sandy, the second child, was so devastated that she ran away from you when she was 12. She also tried to be perfect but was so destroyed that she went through several failed relationships. You see, she can trust no man.

Then there is the third child, Cee Cee. You broke her in with Big Ray and then finished her off yourself. She felt so helpless that she became the wild one, doing the Hollywood scene.

What about your other daughters, your granddaughters and their young friends? Keely? I pray to God that she will remain safe. As you mentioned, Dad, it does make for an interesting story.

Donna

If I had sent that letter to my father, he would have told me that I was mistaken, and he was always right. I was never to question or defy him. That's how the world worked according to Dad, at least Dad's self-made world. It was his way or no way.

Dad kept calling whenever he felt the urge, but if Ken picked up the phone, it would go dead in his hand. I had not answered it for weeks. If we let our answering machine get it, there would be no message. Sometimes it would ring six or seven times in an hour. Always hanging up. There were even calls in the middle of the night.

The weeks of phone calls were wearing me down, and I felt panicky and scared all the time at home. Ken was beginning to lose patience. He still did not understand what was going on, and I was not yet ready to tell him. I didn't want to place my marriage in jeopardy.

During therapy, Rose directed me to make signs and place them next to the phones to help calm me. I printed them in large letters and taped them around my home:

"Poor dear. He is crazy and it's not my problem."

The signs were a good idea at first, but eventually they exacerbated the whole problem. Even when the phone wasn't ringing, the signs reminded me that it soon would. I couldn't sleep for more than two or three hours at a time. My nightmares had become more frequent.

In order to help regain my self-control, I read more books on childhood sexual abuse, hoping to find something, anything, to allay my fears about Keely. During my therapy sessions I kept dragging the discussion back to Keely. Rose still believed that the real issue lay with me and my own childhood abuse. She thought that all of this about Keely was a red herring. I insisted that I was frantic because of Keely. I had nothing concrete to verify my concerns, but I still worried.

I remember once studying the great scientist Hermann von Helmholtz who examined the stages of human thinking. He described the first stage as "saturation," or filling oneself with the contradiction between the problem and the impossible solutions. I had poured over every detail of my childhood. I was indeed saturated with it.

I was afraid for Keely, but I was also afraid of betraying Daddy, of losing him. Surely he would hate me...or kill me. I was afraid of what Ken might do, of what my friends might think...of my children knowing, but my inner voice still would not be quiet

Afraid because of what? Donna, you are developing a strategy.

Am I? The realization that I was indeed toying with a plan startled me. Yes, I felt an idea working its way forth. Helmholtz's second stage was "incubation." My subconscious was struggling to engender a plan. The nightmares and flashbacks were a part of the process.

Donna, you know what you must do. You must ensure that your father never molests Keely...

The answer brought me great relief. I would not sit idly by while Keely was in jeopardy. No, I would do something. I wasn't sure what, but I fantasized an assortment of strategies. The best ones revolved around getting Keely completely safe, but it wasn't easy to do. I could trust neither Cee Cee nor our father. I knew he had guns and was perfectly capable of flying into an uncontrollable rage when crossed. If I got killed, I would not be any help to Keely. To do this right I needed to assemble an army to help me.

I would assemble the troops.

Part IV
Assembling The Troops

No, the past would not stay buried; the skeletons would not stay in the closet.

Over the span of a few short years, my beautiful life had been interrupted more and more often by external events, by revelations of my father's ongoing abuse of those who should have been able to trust him.

As pressure built, the truth took on a life of its own. Even in quiet times, the memories I had so carefully banished to the darkness would rise up, unbidden, to haunt my waking hours and infiltrate my dreams. Flashbacks. Scenes from memory that suddenly take over your consciousness, as if they were happening right now.

I was, more and more, feeling like a victim again, a victim of the past. It went against my grain. Once I had been that helpless child, but I had outgrown helplessness, earned my way out, and I had no desire to play the part of a victim.

My fervent desire was to keep my life on an even keel, but the situation with Keely wouldn't go away. Even keel or Keely? The conflict in my mind made it hard to think. What if Ken left me? What if my children couldn't look me in the eye? What if neighbors never spoke to me again? What if my school district fired me? I had so much to lose, yet something had to be done.

What could I do that wouldn't jeopardize everything I'd worked so hard to build? That wouldn't damage my husband and children? Or our standing in the community, our choices for the future? How could I really carry out what I knew I must to?

As hard as it was to admit it, I knew I needed allies.

October 3, 1989
Rose's Office
Newport Beach

"I think you may be obsessing, Donna," Rose said at our afternoon therapy session. "You may be overreacting to the possibility of danger to Keely. Besides, you're too fragile right now to call Cee Cee and open up this issue."

"But Rose," I countered, "Cee Cee is her mother and needs to protect her."

Rose was adamant: "Donna, please take care of yourself first. You are emotionally weakened and I don't think you're ready for this."

"Maybe I am overreacting," I agreed, but when I got home, I felt so desperate to protect Keely that I dialed Cee Cee's number. She had to be warned. But I only reached a computerized operator saying her number was no longer in service. No new number was available.

I did not feel safe calling anyone else in the family. What if they told Dad what I was saying about him? And if I sent Cee Cee a warning note in the mail, she might show it to him. No matter what she said, Cee Cee was still under his control.

I couldn't resolve anything now. I continued to go through the motions of day-to-day life, but my mind still churned. I hoped a solution would suggest itself.

October 19, 1989
San Juan Capistrano

My mom came down to my house for Saturday morning coffee. She knew I was in therapy and plagued with hang-up calls from my father. She was concerned, having spent so many years trying to figure him out. Mom's fury was still close to the surface about Dad's starting a second family with Bernie while he was still married to her, but I was used to her anger.

This morning we took our cups of hot coffee outside on the patio. It was unusually warm and lovely for October. As we resumed our conversation about Dad's incessant calls, Mom turned and looked directly into my eyes.

"Donnie, did your father ever touch you?" Her voice was level.

When she asked me this before, I had never told her the truth. *Assemble the troops.* I knew that I needed an ally. I hesitated for only a moment, though my pulse was beating wildly.

"Yes, Mom. That's really what this therapy is about. I've been having a terrible time with flashbacks. My therapist says I have acute delayed stress syndrome. It's similar to what Viet Nam vets had after the war. When a person has suffered trauma, years later it can come back to haunt them. It's pretty bad, Mom. I'm having a lot of trouble."

I always suspected that if my mother knew she would flip out, and now I watched her carefully, intent on each nonverbal clue. She went pale and the tears began to flow. Her hands began to shake, and she looked as if she'd stopped breathing.

"Mom, I never told you. I was always afraid it would make you crazy."

"Honey, I asked you before," she cried softly. "Why didn't you tell me a long time ago? Why didn't you tell me so that I could have done something?"

"What would you have done, Mom?" I asked. "You couldn't even get him to stop having Bernie around or stop having children with her." My words became emphatic. "I don't think you could have stopped him."

"Donnie, I won't go crazy. I want to help now." She sobbed, assuring me between sentences. "I always knew he was warped. What can I do? You poor baby. I am so sorry. I never dreamed..." her voice trailed off. "In the last ten years there's been so much more on television and in the papers. I began to worry after his third wife took him to court and had that warrant for his arrest. I heard the rumors." Mother's voice was stronger now.

"I'd forgotten about Crystal."

"What about Sandy?"

"All of us girls, Mom."

"Oh, dear God!"

November 2, 1989
Driving home
San Juan Capistrano

Ken and I were driving home from one of Julie's collegiate soccer games. We were haggard from ceaseless hang-up calls and began to discuss my father. Ken was still very puzzled by Dad's behavior. I knew that soon I must tell Ken. I needed him in my army.

Possibly reacting to intuition as long-married people often do, Ken asked in a tentative voice, "Donna, did your father ever molest you?"

"Yes," I was able to reply without hesitation. I felt I had waded into dangerous waters but I needed his stalwart support. I paused, "It started when I was a little girl."

Ken simply reached for my hand. For the time we each remained silent, letting what I had revealed sink in. His touch reassured me as we drove home, the darkness of the night intensifying our thoughts.

Once we were comfortably seated in our family room at home, Ken heard me out. I had been so afraid of his reaction, but he was immensely understanding, promising me that everything would be okay, that he would protect me.

Much later that night my husband turned to me. I could see the sadness in his face. "Donna, I never said anything all these years, but tonight I have finally come to an understanding." His voice was comforting. "All these years I felt like we were soldiers alone in the world." He paused for a long moment. I could tell this was difficult for him. "There is something else. Any time I came home late from a class or a meeting and tried to touch you in your sleep..." He stopped again.

I wasn't sure if I wanted to hear this. I looked at Ken in the semi-darkness of our family room. My eyes took in the numbers on the digital clock above the television. It was 1:30 a.m. Ken's eyes were large and serious in the dim shadows.

"What, Kenny?"

"Donna, if I ever tried to make love to you in the night..."

"Yes?"

"I could tell you didn't want me."

"Not want you? Kenny, I love you!"

"Donna, it always hurt my feelings so I quit trying. If I would caress your back or touch you, then you would start kicking. Hard. Sometimes you'd even try to bite me. I couldn't figure it out. Sometimes you'd even hiss out in a strange voice, 'No! No! No!' There was such pain in your voice. Then when I'd back off, you'd quiet down and go back to sleep. Donna, I think you were asleep when all this happened."

I was aghast, "Kenny, are you saying that I'd actually yell out 'No'? Oh, dear God..."

My chest constricted and I began to cry as I realized that all my life I had denied the deep, terrible pain that surfaced now. Kenny held me tight.

"Kenny, I'm so sorry."

"Donna, it's okay. I've known something was not right. Now we are one."

We both understood that my fears were a window into the anguish and fury stored in my unconscious. We did not need to say aloud what we understood. Kenny now had the whole garish picture of my childhood. That secret was out.

There was still more for me to tell. Ken had to know about Julie, but that would be another day.

November 4, 1989
San Juan Capistrano

During the next few days, I took my children aside one by one and told them the story of my childhood abuse. They were deeply hurt and angry. Danny and Rick wanted to kill my dad. My precious Julie cried for weeks. When I saw the pain in her face, I began to get a glimmer of the suffering I had frozen inside of me.

The day I told her, we were quietly sipping coffee in the Nordstrom's empty dining room.

"Oh Mom, the safest place I've ever known all my life was in my daddy's arms," she sobbed.

After that she was speechless for a long while. I reflected on Julie's words. Her father's arms had been a secure haven for her.

It was so different in my family. Few of my father's children ever hugged him hello or goodbye. We were always on guard.

Once I had talked with Julie, I knew I could no longer wait to tell Kenny that Dad had touched her when she was ten. My husband had been so good, so understanding when he learned about me. What would he do when he heard about Julie?

When I told Ken, he only asked me a few quiet questions to confirm that Julie was okay; needing to convince him that it really was not more than I had told. Then he got into his truck and left, looking sad and hurt. I was afraid of what he might do, but I was powerless to stop him. He was gone for several hours. When he returned, he seemed very controlled and determined. He simply said he would take care of everything.

Later that night, he told me that he had taken a large hammer from the tool shed and headed for Dad's house in Los Angeles. His plan was to use the hammer to see that Dad never hurt anyone again. On the way there, he fought through his tears of pain and anger enough to achieve some level of rationality.

Just before the off-ramp to Venice, he stopped on the freeway, realizing that attacking Dad physically could result in more problems for all of us. Ken would end up in jail and our lives would be ruined. He turned around and came home, determined to find a way to make the system deal with my father.

Ken knew there was more than one kind of hammer.

November 6, 1989
San Juan Capistrano

Months of sleepless nights and the stress of my full-time teaching activities were beginning to take their toll. This had to end. Then, in the middle of the night, with thoughts colliding in my mind, I finally realized what I must do. Although I was physically tired, my emotional energy was waxing again, thanks to the support of Mom, Ken, and my children. Getting the truth out into the open gave me strength.

I leaped from my bed and began typing a letter to Cee Cee. I had listened to her years before, but I had never confided in her. Cee Cee had to know just how dangerous Dad really was. I had to tell her my story.

I wrote for two hours, pouring out everything I could remember about what Dad had done to me, from my first day of school until I moved into the sorority house. I told her how I had felt dirty and inadequate under my cheerful veneer, and how hard I'd always worked at pretending we were normal. I explained my need to be perfect, to be quiet to protect Ken and my children from scorn and ridicule.

By the end of this letter, Cee Cee knew about my therapy and about the textbook definition of pedophiles who abuse children well into their 70s. I pleaded with her to protect her precious daughter.

"Cee Cee," I wrote, "I want Keely to experience her innocence, to feel clean. I don't want her to have crabs when she is 13 or have nightmares about getting molested. I don't want her to die of shame because she is not a virgin."

As I wrote I felt so much love for my half-sister and her little girl. My mind and heart worked in unison to say the words that would finally bring truth and healing to our family.

"I know that in toxic families everyone has secrets that keep them isolated. Let us not stay so far apart in a lonely, distrustful world."

It was the kind of letter you might write to clear your mind, with no intention of sending. But the next morning I tucked it into an envelope and sent it off with the mailman. No matter the consequences, Cee Cee needed that letter. I knew it beyond a shadow of a doubt.

November 14, 1989
San Juan Capistrano

Kenny answered the phone when Cee Cee called. She was almost incoherent.

"Kenny, I got Donna's letter," she cried. "I'm scared. Dad said you and Donna have been trying to get custody of my kids."

"Cee Cee," Ken's voice was warm but emphatic. "There is no way in the world we want to take your kids. Donna is just very concerned about Keely's safety."

"I know that now, Kenny." Tears choked off her words. "I really believed Dad though. I wanted to believe him. I did not want to think that he would hurt Keely, but I know now that it's true!"

"Kenny, I tricked Dad today to test Donna's letter. I didn't want to believe her. She wrote that she thought Keely was in extreme danger. So I went to Dad's house. While I was cleaning, I told him in my best acting voice, 'Dad, I can live with it if you just touch Keely, but you mustn't do anything else with her." Kenny, I expected him to say that it was all lies." Cee Cee's voice broke for a moment and she paused.

"But, Kenny, he said, 'Coach her for me. Coach her.' He wanted her to not tell their secret. Then I knew that Donna was telling the truth. I grabbed Kyle and Keely and got out of there as fast as I could. I have tried all evening to call you. The phone was busy. I told myself that I would try one more time and you answered."

"Cee Cee you have to come down here right away. Can you come tonight?" Ken was gentle but firm.

"Ken, I'm so afraid. I didn't want to believe it, but Dad says he's going to destroy Donna. He also threatened Chad's life last week. His own son! Daddy kept squeezing the gun that he keeps under the front seat of his car and ranting about Chad. Do you think he would kill Chad?"

"Cee Cee, can you come down here right now?" Ken's voice was urgent.

"I could come tomorrow with Rand and Anne."

"Do that, will you? We'll figure out what to do. We care very much about you, Cee Cee, and we've got to protect Keely." Ken paused to let that message sink in. "Be strong. You did the right thing to call us. You'll be okay." His words were powerful and directive. "Listen to me. Do not answer the telephone, leave the machine on. Keep Keely safely inside the house. You'll be okay. Have you told Rand?"

"He knew that I had been molested before we got married when I was a child, but he doesn't know anything of what's been going on."

"We'll get into it tomorrow. He has to be told." Ken was fierce.

"Now, do as I say. Lock the doors, lock the gate and put the answering machine on."

"Okay. Thank you, Kenny," Cee Cee was quieting down.

Ken hung up and turned to me.

"Donna, she's petrified. That bastard actually convinced her that you were after her kids!" My husband shook his head in disbelief.

I remember the ominous words of Dad's poem: "The troops, nearly always innocent of the nature of war march boldly forth to the beat of the drum."

This was war.

November 18, 1989
San Juan Capistrano

Rand and Cee Cee arrived with their 21-year-old daughter, Anne, four-year-old daughter Keely and baby Kyle. Their sons, Jesse, Russ and Nick, were staying with friends. Cee Cee busied herself in my kitchen putting together the take-out hamburgers she had bought for all of them. Anne got me alone and told me about their trip down to our house.

"Donna, we barely got my mom here. At every off ramp she had an excuse as to why we should turn back. She was crying the whole time. Rand doesn't know what is going on. We'll have to tell him soon. Mom was afraid of what he might do if she told him without your help."

After the hamburger debris was cleared and the children were settled quietly with toys, we took our seats around my dinette table and waited for Ken to get home. Sandy came over for a few minutes to lend moral support.

Cee Cee began, "I told Donna in 1985. I wanted her to stop him then, but she was such a wimp. She didn't do anything."

"I told her in 1981. She didn't do anything then either," Sandy accused.

"Hey, wait a minute," I interrupted angrily. "I'm not the mother here. You two are both adults. I am not in charge of your lives. Don't put this on me!"

I very much resented having the blame laid at my feet. The months in therapy had certainly taught me that all of these people were not my responsibility. My responsibility lay with myself and my own children. I was not about to accept this guilt trip. Sandy had called the authorities years ago but it had done no good. They said they didn't have a case. Also, I had specifically told Cee Cee years before to get away from Dad, and get a job. Instead, she had another child.

"Look, this isn't getting us anywhere," I added trying to stay calm. "We always seem to avoid placing the blame where it belongs...on Dad. Let's get a clear perspective on this thing and decide what we're going to do." I looked around the table at the three women.

"I'm not here to listen to all the gory details," Sandy inserted sternly. "I went through them years ago in therapy and I don't want to get into it again. I just want you to know that you can get well. I went to therapy for three years because of what dear old father did to me. After so many failed relationships with men, I had to learn to trust and learn how to be a girl. My big defense was to act like a tough boy. I'll be your inspiration, and I'm here for support always, but I can't get into it again. I have to leave."

Cee Cee, Anne, and I looked at her. She was confident and straightforward. She seemed strong and sure of herself.

"I do have to go now. I have work tomorrow," Sandy added with a sad smile. "Cee Cee, I'm proud of you for coming down here. You've taken the first step toward getting better."

After Sandy left, Anne and Cee Cee began talking at once. Rand was busy with the baby in the other room, and we decided not to tell him about Dad and Keely yet. We knew we should wait until Ken got home from his meeting to help handle Rand's certain fury.

"Donna, it had been a nightmare." Anne confessed sadly. "I finally told Mom when I was 16. Since then he hasn't come near me, but she's been protecting me with herself."

Cee Cee interrupted, "Donna, he just won't leave me alone. I feel like I'm in prison. He comes by our house and honks every night at the dinner hour. We've tried ignoring him, but he just honks and honks the car horn until it drives us crazy! Last night it went on for two hours. We turned out all the lights and hid on the floor. The phone rang with hang-up calls all day long. He's driving us crazy."

"Cee Cee, I got those hang-up calls for weeks. Whenever someone would answer, he would hang up. I know he was waiting for me to answer, but I never did. I tried to call you a few weeks ago. I would have written sooner but I thought you'd show the letter to Dad and I was afraid of what he might do." There was a long silence.

"Donna, I'm so ashamed. I did tell him you said that he molested you when you were little. He said that was 'a big load of crap' and that he worked hard then and did not have the time. Didn't have time! Pretty weird answer. I also told him some other things about your letter. I'm so sorry." Sobs wracked Cee Cee's slender body as she realized that she had put me in danger.

After several minutes she continued, "Dad convinced me that you really were after the children. He told me to run to Phoenix. Jesse told me two years ago that he saw Grandpa doing things...and I didn't do anything about it then, I thought Jesse would get killed. Dad had me so scared of him."

"Mom and I sat very quietly with Keely yesterday," Anne explained slowly. "After a long while we got her to tell us what Grandpa has been doing to her. It's really terrible. He has had her in the bathtub licking him. He has licked her. She told me about his lips. She said that when he would take her out to breakfast, he would sometimes put his tongue in her mouth while they were sitting in the car. When they went inside the restaurant, she said that Grandpa would put his fingers inside her panties."

"Honey, we must protect Keely. This has to stop." I spoke firmly, my heart breaking inside because of what I was hearing. What had I worried about happening in the future was already true now. I felt sick.

People knew about the abuse and Keely still wasn't safe. Why wouldn't anyone stop him? Donna, you will stop him!

"Dad ordered me not to write to you. He saw me mailing that card to you and challenged me. I told him you were such a sicko that I would send you a get-well card. I even made a mean face about you. He liked my sarcasm and let me mail it. He didn't see the inside. He's after you, Donna, He said, 'If it takes my last two hundred thousand dollars, I'm going to destroy her.' He said he'd hire detectives and also plant some at City Hall to say terrible things about Ken so that he will have to leave office. I don't know what he might do, Donna."

"I'm scared, too," Anne admitted. "The worst was when we were little. Diedre, Connie, the boys and I would all run for the car when it was time to go somewhere. The boys were bigger and would always beat us to the car, but we girls ran frantically. It didn't matter if you had to go to the bathroom or needed a drink of water, or couldn't find your new doll, you just ran. The one who was the slowest was the one who got molested that day while the others waited in the car."

Shivers of terror went through me. Those poor little girls. What kind of human being would do such a thing? My inner voice responded, *Only a very evil one. A very evil one...*

"Donna, Dad has been driving me crazy with that poem he wrote to you. He kept making us all read it. It seemed like gibberish to me, but he insisted that we praise him for it. He was also going off about that letter Sandy read to him last month. He tore it into a thousand pieces and flushed it down the drain."

"That letter," I responded, "detailed the harmful effects of Sandy's abuse and told him to stop abusing everyone else. Sandy needed to confront him for her own healing."

"So what did Sandy do?" Cee Cee looked at me in wonder.

"It was on Halloween. She made a lunch date with him at Marie Callender's restaurant to confront him. She did it all herself. She was very brave. She read him a prepared four-page document, confronting him with it all. Dad's only denial was, 'I didn't love Diedre too much.' Sandy listed all of us in the letter as well as Crystal's daughter, Jaime. She said that his eyes clouded up with tears a few times and at the end he said, 'I made a wrong decision.' That was all of an apology Sandy got. Dad started sidetracking then and blaming everything on our mother. He was very eager to get away from Sandy."

We looked at each other for a long time. This was one of the only planned confrontations Dad had ever had to face for his acts. Was there hope of stopping him?

"When he told me about meeting Sandy," Cee Cee sighed, "he said Sandy just told him to take better care of himself."

"He left out the part about Sandy confronting him with sexually molesting everyone, didn't he?"

Cee Cee nodded her head, "Actually Dad has become pretty weird. One night when he was over, I left the living room for a moment. When I came back in, that vase you painted for me was shattered. He told me that Kyle had crawled over and knocked it down. 'You don't want her shit around here anyway.' He said. I didn't believe him for a second. Kyle never went near that table."

The sound of Ken's truck interrupted us, and I ran to the door to meet him. When he hugged me, I whispered that we had not told Rand yet. Ken understood that we needed him and hurried to join our tense little group. He gave Cee Cee his full support as she told Rand the painful facts.

Rand flew into a rage when he learned that Dad was molesting his wife and child and thundered at Cee Cee, "How could you leave our little girl with him, knowing he was a child molester? How could you?"

Cee Cee cried and begged Rand not to leave her. He was so furious he wanted to go kill Dad. Ken grabbed him by the arms to get him to sit down and finally calmed him enough so we could talk it through.

The night went on interminably, filled with tears and shouting. At last Rand and Anne convinced us to report Dad to the authorities. Cee Cee and I were terrified at the thought, but knew that we must do it. I looked into her eyes and nodded yes.

My inner voice was strong: *Donna, you must protect the children.*

Part V
Launching The Battle

The Chinese tell us that the longest journey begins with a single step, but they fail to tell us how horrifying it can be when that step means certain warfare. Someone will be damaged. Perhaps everyone.

Between our decision to take action and our first real concerted step in that direction, our family members seemed to face a gulf as wide as forever. What we did next transported us into a new dimension, and as terrifying as it was, turned us from victims to warriors. We couldn't predict the outcome, or be certain we would win, but the tide really turned in our souls the day we took that step.

In many ways it seemed worse. I didn't lose my fear overnight; my flashbacks continued. Sometimes I'd even wake up dreaming that I was having one of those friendly phone calls with Dad when he asked about my children and how the dogs and horses were. It was hard to keep track of time.

But in the depths of my being, the part of me that believes all people should be treated fairly scored a great victory when that first step was taken.

At the time, however, I wasn't so sure.

November 17, 1989
Early Morning
Santa Monica

In the gray overcast of early morning we met at Cee Cee's home in Santa Monica. All of my brothers and sisters were there except Connie. We hid our cars around her neighborhood in case Dad drove past the door. We held an emotional family conference led by Ken, and then traveled in small groups the few miles to Stuart House, a center for sexually abused children.

As I sat on the vinyl sofa in the waiting room, I could not help but reflect on the stories I had been hearing from my family all day. One of the girls had slept at Dad's one night. She was a flat-chested little child, ill with the flu, awakened and raped by my father. She described how sick she had been and that sex was dry and dreadfully painful. I was hearing examples of greater violence than I had ever known at his hand. I had never been beaten, locked out naked or whipped with a belt after being raped while Dad yelled, "Whore."

It was almost more than I could stand. For more than four decades I had protected myself by moving to my intellect, where I did not have to feel. I now switched to that more peaceful channel in my mind and tried to be analytical. What kind of a person was Dad really, I wondered? One book I had read stated bluntly that serious legal consequences are not generally imposed on incestuous abusers.

Nothing much is done because our culture recognizes a man as the head of his family, the king of his domain. I remembered reading one story about a man arrested for incest. As they handcuffed him, he turned to the officer and said, "This is some country where you can't even raise your own fuck."

I had also learned that daughters and stepdaughters typically are the victims. The abuse usually begins early, preschool through about age 11, and average cases include all of the daughters. The books also told me that incest is the most common form of child abuse and that 85% of all crimes committed against children are sexual in nature.

Incest represents abuses of power and loss of control. An incestuous father wields absolute authority over a relatively powerless wife and children. Child molesters frequently feel justified in using their daughters. Occasionally a therapist could get an offender to acknowledge the harm done to his victim but he would still feel no real remorse.

The interview procedure started with me as the oldest. I joined a detective and our social worker, Lila, in a small one-way-mirrored room. They told me that I would be observed from behind the mirrored wall. It took about 20 minutes to tell my story. I felt icy calm; the kind of calm people must feel as they face a firing squad. There was no more confusion. I was clear about what I had to do and I did it, simply and directly.

Dad pretended to everyone to be kind, loving, caring, honest and concerned. He was charming and clever, a steady earner and a voting citizen. He devoted a great deal of energy to helping all of us pretend he was a "nice daddy." I supposed that Dad was pretending for himself as well. Denial, I had learned, was a major weapon for the offender. He would never acknowledge that he had harmed us. He lived in his own little world.

At Stuart House we learned many things about sex offenders:

1. They seldom plead guilty.
2. Traditional therapy does not cure them, though they will pretend to be cured.
3. There are excessively high rates of recidivism.
4. Chemical sterilization and a type of brain surgery have been effective in curing offenders.
5. Most sex offenders have been molested.
6. About 30% of men molested as children go on to become molesters.
7. Molesters make a decision to molest.
8. Molesters come from all walks of life. They look like ordinary people.
9. Very frequently it is the natural father who molests his own daughter.

My lifelong friend, Leanne, came to lend her support and sat quietly at my side in the waiting room. Her beautiful brown eyes were filled with tears and grief over what she was hearing. Those eyes were a reminder to me that this was indeed real. It was not an awful nightmare I would awake from.

Before we left Stuart House, a case worker scheduled Keely for a physical examination. A doctor would need to check her to see if there had been any scarring or penetration.

After our long day, we all went back to Cee Cee's and brought in Chinese food. It had been a harrowing week without many meals.

Ken and I played with Keely for a long time up in her room. We could feel that she needed our strength. Late in the afternoon she finally told me what Grandpa had been doing to her. She stuffed a handkerchief into her little rosebud mouth and tried to choke herself so that she could not tell. After a long while she spoke. I still felt the sting of her words.

"Aunt Donna, I know what Grandpa is doing," she whispered to me.

"What is that?" I asked casually.

"He is using his finger to make my little pee pee bigger so that his big pee pee will fit in."

Her tone was conspiratorial; it was a secret shared with a trusted aunt. I kept my cool, but the disgust floated up to the surface.

"I know, Keely, but it's not okay for Grandpa to do that with a little girl."

I was sitting on the floor playing with her dolls. Keely folded herself a bit unsteadily into my arms and leaned her head against my shoulder for a long time. I could feel her terror and understood that for now, I was her strength. I waited all evening, until she was ready for bed before we left.

"Honey, you were something today. You were so strong and so good with Keely. You are my miracle, Donna," Ken spoke softly, holding me against his chest, still damp from his shower. "I thought you were incredible all those years, but I really had no idea."

We turned out the lights. It had been a long day, and I had to teach the next morning. I lay in the dark and tried to recall what psychologist Alice Miller had said about trying to find witnesses who would not be afraid to stand up for children. She had come to the conclusion that their numbers were few. She maintained that society had betrayed its children and begged her readers to protect children from adult's abuse of power.

Alice, it is very scary...

Thanksgiving Day, 1989
Mammoth Lakes, California

We all left town for the holiday; Ken and I took our family to our mountain condominium at Mammoth and Cee Cee and Rand took their brood to Phoenix. The complicated and lengthy police procedure had us hiding out.

Cee Cee called, sounding upset. Keely had stopped breathing the night before. "She was purple. It scared me to death!"

"How is she today?" I was trying to be calm.

"She seems fair, but I had to scream at her to breath. It was so horrible. We got her back to sleep about half an hour later. She cried for a while."

"How about you? How are you holding up?"

"I can't sleep much. Rand is still angry. Donna, if the police don't do something, I'll never feel safe to leave my house again! It was horrible keeping Keely out of school last week and this week. I'm not sending her back until Dad's in jail. When she freaked out last night, it was over a nightmare that Dad would come into the school yard to get her and steal her away. She panics every time she sees a car like his. It could be a long winter."

"I know. I'm even careful where I park. I know Dad keeps an arsenal."

"Donna, recently he bought a semi-automatic. I think he keeps it in the car."

"Tell me how Keely's physical exam went." I was very concerned about my niece.

"The doctor said there was no physical damage. But Keely liked the doctor and told her everything. The doctor couldn't tell me much because of the investigation, but she did volunteer to testify for us. She said she was sickened by what Keely had told her.

"Stuart House made Rand and me and the kids all agree to come in for therapy. They had us sign an agreement. The therapy is free; it's part of their rape program. Rand isn't eager to talk to a stranger. Neither am I for that matter, but I've come this far. I will go through with it."

"We all need therapy. It has really helped me to have an objective person to talk to. Our crazy family rules have brainwashed us. Could I talk to Keely for a minute?"

Keely's sweet little voice came on the line. It warmed my heart. She sounded happy and rushed to tell me about her morning.

"Aunt Donna, Aunt Donna, thank you for loving me. I'm playing horsey now with my other Grandpa."

"It sounds like you are having loads of fun!" I encouraged her. It relieved me somewhat to hear her sound so carefree this morning.

"I am! I've gotta go now! Bye-bye!" Rand's parents loved Keely dearly. She adored playing with this Grandpa. The thought that Keely's trusting little soul had not been safe with my own father filled me with rage.

December 3, 1989
Rose's Office
Newport Beach

When I met with Rose for therapy, she noticed I was in a better mood. I had been granted my sabbatical leave request for the next year. I'd have the entire year off from teaching to study.

"I feel like my life is getting slightly back to normal," I told her. "The misery you've heard from me recently is not at all representative of my whole life." Our eyes met. "I guess hanging out in denial for 40 years did allow me to feel happy much of the time." I paused for a quick moment. "I know that I have been involved on a deep level with others. I have devoted my energies to my children, my husband, and my students. I had not really been concerned about my *self*. I know you think my commitment to my portraiture had helped me cope."

"I believe that you have alleviated much of your fury through your artwork," Rose agreed. "You have been painting for 11 years. That's almost half of your adult lifetime. Look at your paintings a little more closely. They aren't just paintings, are they?" Rose paused, gathering her thoughts.

"Your paintings are almost always portraits of innocent little girls. You have been trying to protect them by preserving their innocence through your brush. I have believed all along that your artwork has saved your life, at least your sanity. It has allowed you a break from the conflicts you feel."

"I unconsciously put myself into art therapy, didn't I?" My response had been a new awareness.

"Yes. You were able to find a way to take care of yourself. Donna you deserve credit for what you have done. You could have discovered alcohol or food. Many do, you know," Rose continued, "You deserve credit for what you have achieved. You have had a loving 26-year marriage, and three very successful, happy children. That alone is a significant accomplishment. Your family system with your husband and children seems healthy. You owe yourself recognition for this. You didn't perpetuate the dysfunctions or the abuse. You've done all you could to stop the cycle. You need to be proud."

I stared at Rose silently, thinking about her analysis of me, of my life.

"And we haven't even gotten to you as a teacher or artist or businesswoman," Rose spoke with conviction.

I wondered briefly how many of my artist friends realized how much we mood alter when we take up our palette and brush? I knew that creativity was a safe harbor for me. I wanted to think more about all of this.

What really brought human happiness? The doing, the creative process, involvement with others. I didn't have time for that idea right now, but something was there to examine. I knew I had made a conscious decision early to be happy. For me the glass had always been "half full."

"Rose," I began a moment later, "I think I have led a rather charmed life, except for one little problem..." I smiled at her, trying to make a joke. I knew that sexual abuse was devastating, but I'd had a good life.

"Perhaps it is only denial," I added, not believing my own words, "and I have had a miserable life. But mostly I have always felt happy. I love being a mom and having a family."

Rose was not saying much. She was ill and I could tell she did not feel well.

Rose's lids were getting heavy. I wasn't sure if she heard me. I continued anyway, hoping that she would snap back.

"Over the 25 years that I've been a mother, I can hardly even think of unpleasant times. I loved it all: the trips to the orthodontist, the dancing lessons, the soccer games, and the family wrestling matches on the living room floor, the birthday parties, the ski trips and the summers at Catalina. It had felt like a grand and marvelous party, and I was center stage helping to direct it. I made my life what I dreamed it would be. That cannot all be denial, can it?"

"Take credit for doing a good job, Donna. And begin to be nicer to the little 'you' inside. She's been locked away for a very long time. When you told me last time that you could not stand to look at pictures of yourself from ages five through twelve that means you've not been acknowledging that brave little girl. She needs credit for surviving what she survived and growing into the kind of person she has."

I replied, "I'm ashamed of her. She feels pain and she's all needy and screwed up. I like to keep her locked up. She bugs me." I meant it. "I can't stand to look at my childhood pictures."

"To get better, you're going to have to let her out and feel her pain and then learn to love her and take care of her. You must learn to be as good to her as you have always been to your children. You wouldn't lock them up, would you?"

"Certainly not!" I answered too quickly. Rose gave me a look that said, "Well then?" We sat without speaking for a long interval.

After a moment Rose asked, "Donna, your family means a lot to you, doesn't it?"

"They mean everything to me!" I thought of Keely, only a defenseless little girl. I would do anything to protect the children. I knew it wasn't over yet. I was in danger. Nothing was settled.

Rose continued, "I am very serious when I say that you deserve credit for what you have done."

My comfortable moment had passed. I heard Rose's words, but they were just noises scratching against my eardrums. I was still caught up in a war against my father. My family was in danger.

December 15, 1989
Cee Cee's Home
Santa Monica

Today the detective wired Cee Cee to record her conversation with Dad. She was to make a breakfast date with him so that police could get some more evidence for the trial.

Ken was trying to hold her together. He had gone to her house early in the morning to be there when the police arrived. Cee Cee was frantic with fear. She could not believe she had committed herself to having breakfast with Dad. Did he know we had all gone to the police? Was he planning to set her up? Would he shoot her, and then turn the gun on himself?

Rand was trying to keep the kids from driving their mother crazy. They had been home for weeks, too frightened to go to school. Everyone was on edge and irritable.

Cee Cee started calling our father's house at eight o'clock to make the date. No answer. She tried every 20 minutes for three hours. The police stayed with Cee Cee while Ken disguised himself as a bum in an old overcoat and baseball cap, and went to see whether Dad was home. He drove close to the house, parked and walked around the front of the property. The drapes were drawn shut. Dad's car was in the carport. He was there.

Ken called back to Cee Cee's from his cellular phone to report. Cee Cee dialed Dad's number again and again. No answer. Did he suspect something? Was he ill? Was the phone unplugged?

By one o'clock our brother, Trey, reported that Dad had called him. Dad was going to the bank with Diedre, our youngest sister, and was leaving town for Florida in the morning. The police left. They told Cee Cee and Ken that they would try another time. We knew this failure to get more evidence would put off the arrest for weeks.

The detective assured Ken and Cee Cee as he left her house that an arrest would be made after Dad's return from Florida. There were still some details he was concerned about. He had wanted something on tape. The warrant for Dad's arrest was drawn up and waiting to be implemented. We were asked to be patient.

Later in the day Trey was able to communicate again with Dad. Trey told Dad that Cee Cee was very sorry for ignoring him lately, that she had been upset about money. He got Dad to agree to call her at nine o'clock the next Friday morning.

December 28, 1989
Cee Cee's Home
Santa Monica

Keely sat quietly in the arms of her Uncle Trey, listening to the story he was reading her. After a while she turned her face up to him.

"I'm going away soon."

"Going away? What do you mean, you silly girl?" he teased.

"I'm leaving."

Trey tried to get more from her, but she wouldn't talk. He felt frustrated, but managed to read the story to her.

Later Trey reported the odd remark to Cee Cee and Anne.

Cee Cee spoke softly, "Yesterday she told me that she was sorry she had caused all this trouble. She's been soiling her pants many times a day lately. I'm really worried about her."

Anne chimed in, "Mom, two days ago I had to break into the bathroom while she was having one of those privacy baths her therapist wants her to have. I knocked and knocked and called her name. She wouldn't answer. I was alarmed and finally used a hairpin to pick the lock. Keely had filled the tub almost to overflowing. I yelled, 'Keely, what are you doing? You didn't answer me!' She just gave me the weirdest, most detached look. All she said was, 'I was practicing,' Mom, I didn't know what she was talking about. It kinda spooks me."

"Yesterday, she wanted to know exactly what day Grandpa would be back from his trip to Florida. I told her probably on Saturday. She was terrified." Cee Cee's eyes filled with tears. "You don't suppose she is thinking of ..."

"Killing herself..." Anne said in a low monotone. "She is thinking of killing herself."

Cee Cee, Anne and Trey were stricken. Could it be possible that little Keely was thinking of suicide? Was she going to try to drown herself?

December 29, 1989
The Stuart house
Santa Monica

Keely was given an emergency appointment at Stuart House. After talking in length with Trey and Anne, Cee Cee was convinced that Keely was suicidal.

That night, Cee Cee telephoned me in the evening certain that this day with Keely would go down in her life as the most tragic and bizarre she would ever experience.

Keely and Cee Cee had joined Nora, a therapist, in the children's private therapy room. Keely had immediately begun to run around and around the room, hitting at toys and boxes, breaking everything as she ran.

"Donna, Nora and I sat in these little chairs while Keely slapped at the wall and knocked stuff around. Her eyes were glassy and she was breathing really fast. Nora said she was hyperactive, hyperkinetic. When Keely finally stopped breaking things, she ran over and started to beat on Nora's chest and face with her fist. She hit her so hard that she knocked Nora over in her chair. Nora didn't resist. She just took the beating." Cee Cee sounded exhausted.

"Then while Nora was struggling to get out of the tiny plastic chair and right herself, Keely climbed into the toy cabinet. We tried to coax her out, but there was no response. She stayed in there for more than an hour. It was awful. I've never seen Keely like that."

"Finally Nora got the idea to coax her out of the closet with walkie-talkies. Well, that did it. Keely slowly came out. It was absolutely surreal. After eight hours, Nora was finally able to get past Keely's anger and fear by talking on the walkie-talkies. By late afternoon Keely came into Nora's arms and hit her again. Then she just fell into a helpless little ball and cried and cried. She said, 'I don't hate you, Nora. I love you.' It was such a nightmare. And that bastard father of ours doesn't think he has hurt any of us!"

"Nora told me that suicide is common, even among very young children like Keely. It is statistically measurable for six-year-olds. Donna, Nora explained that Keely feels suicidal because she 'told' on Grandpa with her Barbie dolls last week. Nora feels that Keely is so fearful about what her grandfather will do to her for telling that she would rather die than deal with her fear of him."

"Last week Nora said that she and Keely played dolls nicely in the therapy room When Nora introduced the grandpa doll, Keely took it, went into the closet and shut the door. Nora called through the door to her. 'Keely why are you in there?' Nora said she finally answered back. 'Nobody must know. It's a secret.' A while later Keely came out of the closet, Nora tried to get her to explain. All she would say was, 'It's a secret.' The dolls were naked. Keely had taken off their clothes."

I was shaken. "Cee Cee, what are we going to do? Can I help?"

"Nora said not to leave her alone for more than a minute at a time. No more privacy baths. I'm moving Russ's bed into her room for now so she won't be alone at all. Donna, I just can't believe this is happening to my little Keely." Cee Cee was heartbroken.

After I hung up the phone, I made myself a cup of chamomile tea and took it into my blue living room. I needed quiet and peace just to think. As I sipped the soothing brew, I tried to visualize Keely's alarming behavior. I had come to understand that I had frozen those feeling long ago because they were too painful to deal with. At five, how could I have lived with mortal fear and love of my caretaking father? I could not have.

I had insight into mental illness, some understanding of the enormous burden of carrying around such tremendous emotion, such conflicting feeling and pain. "Going crazy" could be a way out of the pain for some people, but most of us freeze the feelings. We stuff them far away behind our protective wall of denial. Witnessing Keely's terror illustrated, in a way that books could not, exactly how intense the fears were that I had locked away.

My glance caressed the room. I loved this room. Country French, quiet and immaculate, it was always a haven for me, but it could not comfort me now. Dad would be back in town in a few days. I was still scared.

December 29, 1989
San Juan Capistrano

Sleep continued to elude me. I thought about many things in the night, about little Keely, about how phobic I had always been about incest.

I had been an incest victim, but until recently I could not even use the word. Now I knew volumes about sexual abuse. I knew that sexual abuse was generational. I knew that my grandfather and grandmother were perpetrator and victim. There were four affected generations that I knew of in my family.

It was almost more than I could believe. I stared out of my window into the night for a long time, my stomach knotted. The darkness reminded me of a disturbing book by Dr. M. Scott Peck, *People Of The Lie*. This psychology book, written by a medical doctor, gave me much to ponder about my family. Even his introduction alarmed me:

> THIS BOOK IS A DANGEROUS BOOK. I have written it because I believe it is needed. I believe that the overall effect will be healing...But I have also written it with trepidation. It has potential for harm. It will cause some readers pain.

Dr. Peck was correct with that point. It had given me pain. It forced me to consider possibilities that I had never dared to embrace; ugly, monstrous possibilities. I allowed my mind to consider some of what I had recently read:

Psychiatrists call them psychopaths or sociopaths... people utterly lacking in conscience or superego. Psychopaths appear to be bothered or worried by very little – including their own criminality. They are sometimes referred to as "moral imbeciles."

This is hardly the case with those I call evil. Utterly dedicated to preserving their self-image of perfection, they are unceasingly engaged in the effort to maintain the appearance of moral purity...While they seem to lack any motivation to be good, they intensely desire to appear "good." Their "goodness" is at the level of pretense. It is, in effect, a lie. This is why they are the "people of the lie."

I was particularly disturbed when Dr. Peck came to a discussion about a patient of his, whom he had labeled as evil. He said that he was overwhelmed to think of what it might be like to be the "child of evil." These thoughts turned my stomach. He also included intrusiveness in his definition of evil:

Intrusive parents do not allow their children personal boundaries. "Love is incomprehensible to evil." Evil people have a desire "to confuse." Their behavior is typified by scapegoating and lying.

I scanned quickly across my life and heard afresh in my memory the sound of my father's voice telling an eternity of lies: "Maymie lost the family money. Cee Cee was dropped on her head. Your mother doesn't want you. Donna is out to steal Cee Cee's children." A shudder passed through me as I continued to read:

> First I have come to conclude that evil is real. It is not the figment of the imagination of a primitive religious mind feebly attempting to explain the unknown.

> People who are evil...hate the light and instinctively will do anything to avoid it, including the attempt to extinguish it. They will destroy the light in their own children and in all other beings subject to their power.

Evil was real? I was so naïve. I had never really considered it before. Was my father evil? I considered that thought for a long time. More pictures and words churned to the surface of my memory. I had to face the truth. *He consistently said that he would destroy you...*

December 30, 1989
Mammoth Lakes

Dad was out of town, so we felt it was safe to leave Cee Cee while we went to Mammoth for a few days. But she needed to stay in touch by phone.

"Donna," she wailed, "He called again tonight. I was so nervous, I thought I would explode. I did my best acting. He seemed to buy it. He railed against you. Said that you're a Nazi and it's your Burwick German blood that would have you turn in your own family."

"He told me again," Cee Cee continued, "that you were after the kids. It was horrible. He said, 'Shut Keely up! It would be catastrophic if she talked!' I got lots of stuff like that on the tape, just like the detectives taught me."

"What happened?" I asked, a million questions coming to mind.

"I started out all confused in the first call. I was Daddy's little nitwit. He bought that one. Then in the second call I still acted confused, but I laid some facts on him. He didn't like that much. I am so scared, Donna."

"Hey, this is your sister here. You think I don't know? You haven't seen me having any big talks with him lately. I'm scared of him, too. Don't apologize. I think you're incredible."

"Well, I hope I didn't sound phony. I kept my voice calm, but I kept hitting him with a few more facts each minute or so. He tried talking about the weather, how terrible you are, that you will get Keely, that I should toss Rand out. Dad kept contradicting himself. He would have been killed in debate class."

"What do you mean?" I was intrigued.

"I kept telling him that this can't keep going on with Keely. He said, 'Nothing happened.' Then pretty soon he said, 'Nothing's going on now because I'm gone.' Can you believe that he incriminated himself like this? Oh yes, there was more of that stuff about conservatorship or guardianship or whatever. He kept going on about it."

"Cee Cee, you remember when Daddy kept threatening to put Maymie away?"

"Yeah, vaguely. It was a long time ago, wasn't it?"

"Probably 20 years ago, but that was one of the first conscious awarenesses of how very scary Daddy really is. I think I always knew that if I told, I would either have an 'accident' on one of our trips, like falling down the Grand Canyon or end up locked away as a nut case. It was very chilling when he was threatening her about that. Conservatorship. He threatened to get her declared incompetent. Who even thinks like that?" I stared ahead lost in my own thoughts for a moment.

"Cee Cee, you used that genius brain in getting him to admit so much."

"That damaged genius you mean?" Her voice was mischievous for an instant. "I got so tired of being called 'some kind of damaged genius.' Well, Dad, I hope you like these tapes." Defiance spiced her words.

"Honey, I doubt that any Hollywood writers could have come up with a better way of drawing him out."

"The police cleared their gear out of here a while ago. They are going to listen to the tapes and see what we have for court. I think it's pretty incriminating."

"Cee Cee, maybe you should be the actress in the family."

"I guess we all have been," she responded. "Just trying to act normal. This episode tonight felt like the final reading for a drama class."

Later we would study the three transcripts carefully. The police used initials describing Dad as RL and Cee Cee as CK. Here are some excerpts:

RL: Oh, Cee Cee, it is her word [Keely's] against her grandpa's word and that doesn't count for much. Those are absolutely horrible people   [Stuart House authorities]. Keely has been very well-treated, dear. But for God's sake keep her away from everybody.

CK: Yeah. Okay.

RL: Don't let anyone near her.

CK: Okay.

RL: If they want to talk to her, tell them you want a lawyer present.

CK: All right. Yeah, well I haven't seen Anne in a few days because the last time I saw her she started talking about you and her.

RL: She had better be quiet. Explain that to her.

CK: Well, that really upsets me, too.

RL: Well, explain that to her. She needs to be quiet.

CK: Well, I will, I will.

RL: She is just making trouble and probably for herself.

CK: Well, the stuff she is telling me, I hope it isn't true.

RL: Of course it isn't true. You have people that would like to put me in a position where they can get custody of my money.

CK: Oh.

RL: This is what some of this is all about. If they could prove I am dumb enough to do these things they are claiming, they could get guardianship over me.

CK: Um hum.

RL: These are not nice people, dear. You shouldn't talk to them. Just keep away from them.

CK: Well, I am trying not to. You know I haven't.

RL: That's the idea. Get a hold of Anne, tell her to put a muzzle on and behave herself.

CK: Well, I am just going to sit here and do the best I can, dodging the calls and stuff then. I don't know.

RL: Oh, dodge them. Coach Keely to say nada. Keely should absolutely say nothing. Donna and Sandy will make you more trouble than you ever believed possible. Donna is trying to get Keely. That is what this is all about.

CK: No, I don't...

RL: Does Rand want them to get Keely? Doesn't he realize that is what they are doing?

CK: No, he...

RL: He opens his big mouth. Doesn't he know he will lose her?

CK: Well, he wants to make sure nothing, you know, nothing weird is going down with his little girl.

RL: Nothing weird is going down.

CK: That is all. He was just...

RL: She is absolutely fine. But if he manages to show that something weird is going down with his girl, enough to satisfy someone, he will lose her.

CK: Yeah, well...

RL: God, what an asshole he is. He must not have brains at all. Anyway the whole thing is dead. Just leave it that way.

CK: Well, I know, but it didn't sound too dead. It sounds like Ken Friess is in there doing something.

RL: Oh, sure, he wants to get a little girl for Donna. He couldn't make her one, so he's gonna take yours away from you.

CK: Oh, God.

RL: Explain to Rand that if he doesn't put a muzzle on Keely and soon, and a muzzle on Anne, that you guys are going to lose your little girl. Donnie will wind up with her.

CK: Yeah, well they are coming and asking me questions you know.

RL: Shut up and don't tell anybody anything!

CK: Rand said he was wanting to have Keely go up there.

RL: Well, explain that by having her go up there...if they find anything, he will lose his little girl.

CK: All right.

RL: You absolutely must say nothing. Anne must say nothing. Keely must say nothing and then there is nothing. Rand must not talk to Donna and Sandy. They are trouble makers. Why does he want to lose Keely?

CK: No, he is just trying to protect her.

RL: Protect her? He is trying to throw her to the wolves. Those are vicious wolves down there. Coach her not to say boo to anybody. You must not say anything to anybody. Let this thing go to sleep.

CK: Okay.

RL: Does Rand realize that he is screwing around with the house you are living in?

CK: I'll talk to him.

RL: I mean, my God, if they put me on the fryer, monster legal fees are going to come up, your house will just absolutely slide away from you, dear. I will be somewhere else. There is no way that you can sit in that house and have me fighting legal battles.

CK: Are you threatening me, Daddy?

RL: You are being threatened by Donna and Sandy. If they get me into some forty or fifty thousand dollar legal battle, it is going to eat your house up. That is what they are trying to do. Get a conservatorship over   me and show that I am enough of a nut to do something like, along those

lines, which I certainly am not. They would like to grab my whole estate   and everything and you would be out on your ass.

CK: All right.

RL: So you have vicious people. Nothing has gone anywhere lately. Things are like they are. Keep quiet. Keep Rand quiet. Have Anne quiet. And everything quiet and everything will be fine.

CK: Keely told me. She told me the same things that I did when I was little. She told me about taking baths and washing pee pees.

RL: Oh God, honey.

CK: And I did that, so I know that she is not lying to me.

RL: No way, honey, no way.

CK: I can't have this happen to Keely.

RL: Oh, of course, nothing is going to happen to Keely. You know, I have obviously given Keely up. You know that. What else? People hadn't turned on me at that point.

CK: People aren't turning on you. People are finally telling the truth. And they are hurt.

RL: Yeah, I am so far out on my own, God.

CK: But you put yourself there. What you have done has divided all of us. You never wanted us to talk about that. It has been the big secret.

RL: It is an unspeakable subject.

CK: It is an unspeakable subject because it shouldn't happen. A man should find a woman, not his own daughters and granddaughters.

RL: It can't happen and I can't be in it. It is unspeakable.

CK: I really honestly feel that things could be all right if you could just maybe…you do need to have some help and therapy.

RL: Oh, honey. That would be nice if they could get me into that kind of position where they give me some help and you know, I get to see the warden and I go into the prison library and so on. Then they rehabilitate me and of course by that time Donnie has all my money, and she has your little girl and everything else. Oh, my God.

CK: You just feel that everybody is out to get your money.

RL: I am weak and sick and, Jesus, I can't even be allowed to die in peace. You know what I mean?

CK: You are not dying.

RL: I am not in the best shape either.

CK: Everybody has put you, all of us, every girl, every daughter, everybody has gone beyond the limits of what a daughter should do to take care of you and love you. The issue is sexual stuff.

RL: There is no sexual stuff, period.

CK: You have done a lot of great things. There is no denying that. You could be a great grandfather and a great father. The only problem is the sexual stuff has to stop.

RL: It has stopped. There isn't any. There never was and it has stopped because I am away. Don't you understand I am not there.

CK: And what happens when you come home?

RL: Nothing...

January 17, 1990
Venice Beach

The black-and-white police car pulled behind Dad's three-story stucco beach-front home early that morning. From the cellular phone inside the police car, the Los Angeles Police dialed my father's number.

"Hello?" I could imagine the youthful quality that would be in Dad's voice as he answered. He would still be sleepy from gambling at the Gardena casino the night before.

"Mr. Landis?"

"Yes."

"It is the police. We have a warrant for your arrest. There are officers in the front of your house and in the back. We want you to come out slowly with your hands up."

The detective reported to me that Dad came out peacefully. He was dressed in slacks and a blue print shirt covered by his black leather jacket.

I felt sorry for my father, regret for what he could have been. He was brilliant, handsome, funny, gifted, charming and talented. But somewhere, somehow, Dad had chosen to follow a forbidden path. He might not have believed in God or sin or heaven or hell, but I knew that the loss of face, the loss of his family and the anticipation of a life of incarceration was going to be a living hell.

I felt a great sadness for all of us. We had all wanted a normal Daddy so much that we tried to turn him into one. It never did work very well. I thought of all the books I had read on psychological games and life scripts. I remembered one explanation that stayed with me.

Dr. Claude Steiner said that one can easily determine a "life script" by its ending. Daddy's life would have a tragic ending, whether he was held in prison for the rest of his life or whether he got out. He had ruined all that was important to him. Maymie's long-ago prophecy was close to target:

"I'm so worried that he will end up a lonely old man in a rented room."

For the time being, his rent would be paid by the State of California.

And what of us? What would all of his children have been had he not raped our minds and bodies? The abandonment and abuse I experienced in my childhood had so colored the fabric of my being that I could not imagine another life, a life without terror or shame, a life anesthetized by accomplishment.

Maybe I would not have achieved all that I had. Maybe I would not have been so driven. I thought about that for a while. Perhaps I would have learned "to be" instead of "to do." Perhaps I would have known peace. Perhaps I will someday. I still have lots of time. The rest of my life.

January 18, 1990
Municipal Court
West Los Angeles

I sat in the spectator gallery of the West Los Angeles Municipal Courtroom and diverted my eyes as the bailiff brought in the prisoner, my father.

All but one of my father's seven children was here to beg the court not to allow him bail. Many of his grandchildren, his son-in-law and even a future daughter-in-law were here, huddled in the back rows of the courtroom, clutching one another's hands and praying that the system would not let him out; praying that Daddy would not get us.

I looked at my siblings, front-line warriors in our gruesome battle. They were brave, wholesome, loving souls. My brothers had a clean-cut, all-American appearance. My sisters were all so different, yet each attractive in her own way.

After a moment I looked across the small courtroom at the handcuffed prisoner...Daddy, the aerospace engineer. Daddy, the president of the yacht club. Daddy, the accused felon. His gaze was fixed straight ahead, his face stretched back into a demonic expression by overzealous plastic surgery. In his typical controlling manner he had ordered the surgeon to pull his face even tighter than the doctor thought appropriate.

With his athletic, muscular build, he looked younger than his 66 years. He wore his favorite leather jacket and a print jersey shirt. His sparse blonde hair was combed over to cover his balding head.

The arraignment proceedings began as the young, slightly rumpled district attorney rose to his feet, straightened his tie, and requested permission to show the judge a receipt for a semi-automatic gun recently purchased by my father. It was a sophisticated weapon, holding twelve rounds.

The judge, a serious-looking, middle-aged woman engulfed in black robes, studied the document placed before her carefully. Her head inclined slightly toward the district attorney as he spoke with her for several minutes.

Thinking about the gun that my father owned, I looked over at Diedre, my youngest sister. She had seen our father only three days before. I remembered what he had said to her.

"Diedre, do you know what they do to people who betray their family? It is the same as for people who betray their country. They execute them."

He had laughed hysterically as he floored his new white Chevrolet convertible and sped away, tires squealing.

How could he have hurt and betrayed us all so terribly? I knew the truth. He was malignantly evil and monstrously manipulative. I knew he had robbed us of our innocence, of our childhoods and of our very basic human dignity. I knew he was a dangerous pedophile, a child molester, guilty of sexually abusing helpless children. I knew he had lied and continued to lie about his actions. I knew he had tried to frighten his adult children with detectives, case workers and attorneys. I knew he swore he was being framed. I knew he would never admit the truth.

As the legal proceedings continued, I turned once again to my internal world, to the painful dialogue in my head. "Daddy's girl! Oh, how proud I had always been to be Daddy's girl. It was always Daddy who took care of you. How could you...?" I interrupted myself. "The 'lips' Donna, remember what Keely told you? The 'lips' and all the rest. No. He is where he must be."

The defense attorney stood to address the judge. My father's counsel was immaculate in his expensive tailored suit as he spoke. The motion he placed before the court was quite brief.

"Your Honor, I request that a $2,500 bail be set," he ended matter-of-factly, waiting for the judge to consider the matter.

I could see the district attorney flex his left fist, clenching it open and closed as the defense spoke. After a moment he stood, appearing incredulous at the low bail requested. Looking slightly disheveled in his sport coat, the young prosecutor began:

"Your Honor, the people request that the accused be held without bail due to the severity of his crimes and the duration of the abuse to his family. The State believes that he is a clear danger to his family.

"Your Honor," he continued, his voice now louder and stronger, "The People realize that this is an extraordinary request. However," he paused, looking for a long moment at the judge, "the severity of the defendant's sexual crimes requires extraordinary measures. The State requests that the prisoner be held without bail. Thank you, Your Honor." He stressed the words "without bail," and a prolonged silence filled the air, all eyes locked on the judge.

The judge paused for a long moment. "Bail denied. The defendant will be remanded to custody," she said gravely, pounding the gavel three times.

Indeed the request was unusual. I only knew of one case recently when the prisoner had been held without bail and that was Richard Ramirez, "The Night Stalker." Even the infamous McMartins, accused of molesting children in their preschool, had been granted bail.

January 25, 1990
Bail Review Hearing
Municipal Court
West Los Angeles

My father's attorney had requested a bail review which the judge granted for one week after the arraignment hearing. Knowing that I could have to testify against my father, all three of my grown children, Rick, Julie and Dan, accompanied me to court.

My children had all been away at college. Rick flew down from law school in San Francisco. Julie and Dan drove up from San Diego. When I arrived, the three of them spotted me outside the courthouse simultaneously. They rushed to me, taking turns wrapping me in their strength.

As we walked inside the courthouse, Rick kept his arm protectively around my shoulders. It was a switch for my children to protect me. I had always been strong for them, but they knew that I needed them now. They were all subdued, though I sensed the ferocity of their anger toward their grandfather just below the surface.

Our group filled the small gallery of the courtroom we had occupied the week before. All of my brothers and sisters were there, except Connie who remained loyal to Dad. Our husbands, my mother, my aunt, my lifelong friend, Leanne, my husband's sister and my youngest brother's fiancée sat in the small gallery of the courtroom.

Ken, my sons, Rick and Dan, my sister Sandy and her husband filled the front row. I tried to hide behind them in my second row seat, clutching Leanne's hand tightly. Julie and Anne clung to each other nearby. I kept my eyes stubbornly toward the floor while Leanne whispered an urgent narration.

"They are bringing him in now. He doesn't look bad. He is walking around to his seat. The bailiff is unlocking his handcuffs." Her voice remained steady as she commented on the scene. My heart was racing furiously as it had the week before.

"The bailiff is cuffing his left hand to the chair." She held my hand tighter. "Don't look, Donna."

I tested myself, checking for strength. I glanced up where I knew the prosecutor would be. I was safe. I kept my gaze on him. He stood. The judge looked at him as the district attorney began.

"Your Honor, the prosecution is here at the request of the defense. The State's position has not changed. We believe that this man is a risk to the safety of his family. Certain family members are afraid of him, and he is at high risk of fleeing. The State requests that 'no bail' status be continued until the preliminary hearing. "

The judge, a calm, intelligent-looking woman, gazed expectantly at the defense attorney. "Present your case then counselor," she demanded.

"Ah, Your Honor," he stumbled, seeming rattled and unprepared. "We do not have a case." A snicker stirred through our group of spectators.

Momentarily, the defender seemed to find more words. "Your Honor, it is the responsibility of the State to prove that this man is a threat to his family and that he has the potential to flee. I would like to remind the court that he has lived in Los Angeles his entire life, has owned property, and has never been arrested before. He had no police record. Therefore, it is up to the prosecution to prove these allegations."

He paused for a moment, looking directly at the judge. "A 'no bail' status is highly unusual for the charges presented against my client."

The judge turned her glance toward the youthful prosecutor. "Sir, are you prepared to present your case?"

"Yes, Your Honor," he responded instantly.

The courtroom was cleared and we were ushered outside to wait in the hall. Within seconds the bailiff called my name. A quick rush of adrenaline charged through my body.

Head held high, I sucked in a breath of air and walked through the short swinging doors which separated the empty gallery from the trial space. I was escorted up to the witness stand and told to raise my right hand.

I knew that my father's eyes were on me. I knew that there would be no turning back. My father had recently called Trey and told him that I was after his money; that I was the "ring leader." My father also called the *L.A Times* and tried to get a reporter to do a story about my framing him. I knew he was raging at me now.

"I do," I responded to the oath.

The bailiff led me to the witness stand. I sat down and she adjusted the microphone to my height. The district attorney had instructed me to simply tell the truth. He promised me that I would be able to explain myself easily and that these proceedings were very informal. He was wrong.

I stated my name, age, occupation, and residence. I tried to tell my story in response to the district attorney's questions. There were so many interruptive objections from the defense that we were getting nowhere. After a while, he tried a different tactic.

"Were you ever molested by this man?"

"Yes." My face did not betray my feeling, but I knew that I had told the secret. I had told, in front of a judge, with my father as a witness. It felt right. In a peculiar way it felt good. It was something that needed to be told a very long time ago.

"At what age?"

"Since I was about six years old."

"Who is he?"

"My father."

"Do you believe that you are in any danger if he is allowed out on bail?"

"Yes."

"In what way?"

"He told my sister Cee Cee that he was going to destroy me if it took his last dollar."

"Objection."

"Sustained."

"Were you ever personally threatened?"

"He threatened me that if I told, I would be a 'sorry sister' and that 'people who told end up six feet under'."

"Does your father own a gun?"

"Yes."

"Have you ever seen it?"

"Yes, on many occasions. He always carried it on our trips."

"No further questions."

The defense attorney stood to begin his questioning. I kept my gaze on the prosecutor as I kneaded the palm-sized fleece teddy bear which my therapist had forced me to take to the stand. Back and forth, I worked it in my left hand, unconsciously squeezing it. I could not look at my father. I knew that to see the fury in his eyes would scare me speechless. I heard the defense attorney's questions, but I did not look at his face. He was a disembodied voice, cold and unfriendly, accusing and mean.

"Isn't it true that Venice is a high crime area?"

"No."

The attorney kept up a rapid-fire flow of questions. "Isn't it possible that your father is getting his car ready to sell to use the funds for his defense?"

"I suppose," I answered, thinking that it was much more likely he was getting ready to leave town. I didn't know if Dad really would come after me if he were released. I did think he would flee.

If he was found guilty, my father faced up to 40 years in jail. It did not take a mental giant to figure that Dad would be more than 100 years old when his sentence was complete. Over the years, he had frequently talked about living in the South Sea Islands or in Mexico. As the defense attorney continued his interrogation of me, I could feel a memory struggling to work its way up. It seemed jagged around the edges, sharp and ugly, trying to burst forth.

I remembered now. Daddy was holding me, crooning softly to me about how wonderful it would be for us to be together, married, in the South Pacific where no one would ever take me away from him.

It always scared me the way he said things like that. I could still easily remember his silky smooth words. My stomach flopped over. I could see that faraway dreamy look he would get. I had been afraid he might steal me and take me away where I wouldn't see my mom or Sandy or my grandparents ever again.

Yes, my father would flee if he were released. With his savings he would be rich in Mexico and could look for another young girl.

"That is all. You may step down. Thank you."

I sensed that the judge was speaking to me. I tuned back into the present and looked at the prosecutor. His face told me with a minuscule movement that I had done well. I made my way past the little swinging gate to the outside of the courtroom.

"Sandra Stevens." I heard the bailiff as she called my sister.

Two of my sisters, Sandy and Cee Cee, testified after me. The judge considered all of our testimonies, and at the end of the day announced her decision.

"The defendant will be remanded to the Los Angeles County Jail without bail."

February 17, 1990
San Juan Capistrano

Waiting for the preliminary trial was agony. It could still be several months away. I was reeling from hour to hour in ambivalence. In the early months, I had so much indignation and anger that I was able to fend off the sadness. But these days it found its way into my heart like radioactive gases must have found their human targets, leaking silently out of Chernobyl, oozing forth their unmerciful poisons.

The ooze mostly attacked in the night; I awakened dreaming of lying in a pool of blood or hearing Daddy's voice coaxing me, "Stop this now! Stop this!" Or I woke up in a panic from a nightmare where I was running, being chased, a killer stalking me. Running. Once, I was locked out.

It all left me feeling sad.

I flopped back and forth between knowing what must be done and wanting to run away. One part of myself reminded me that it was not acceptable to molest little children, while the other part said, "Let it go. Let it be. He is your daddy, for God's sake!" Bernie had even been telling my sisters, "Donna and Ken are overreacting. You shouldn't, any of you, be doing this. You turned out alright. What he did didn't really hurt you."

I worried all the time that the story would find its way to the news, and my family's entire sordid tale would be broadcast before the world. I could visualize myself covering my face as they led me to a long dark car outside of the Santa Monica Courthouse. I could see myself holding my purse in front of my face so no one would know that this was about me. But sadly, a small part of me simply missed my dad.

February 20, 1990
San Juan Capistrano

During a day of boating in San Pedro Harbor, I found myself painfully missing Dad. Returning home that evening, I replayed the telephone messages. Trey's voice, youthful and crisp on the recording, reported that he had spoken with Dad.

"Donna, Dad says this is all a frame-up, all lies. That you are after his money. He's hiring a detective. He says he's going to subpoena Cee Cee's therapist records and prove that she is crazy. Call me. There's more." The machine beeped off. My heart throbbed against my rib cage. I felt nauseous, stupid. To think I had been missing my dad!

Donna, you are a stupid fool. You've been taken in your whole life. Dad wants to destroy you. Would probably kill you if he could and you want to take him for a little family boat ride! Stupid. Stupid. Stupid. My inner voice was screaming at me; it wouldn't let up.

*And while you're at it...*my blood was coursing, turbocharged with fear and anger, as I digested Trey's call. My critical inner voice would not be ignored. *Remember back when Julie was about 10? You can't stuff that anymore. Remember...helping her put her Barbies away in her room, and she turned to you, huge eyes luminous in the dim light? They were filled with fear. Terror even. Do you remember her whispers to you?*

Remember? You could hardly hear her? What did she say? My critical inner self mocked me.

Yes, I remember. "Please, I don't want to remember!" I begged my tender inner self. No. Dear God. I do not want to remember...

Remember and know what you are dealing with.

I stared out the window. The view was lovely. The sun was setting and the sky was a blaze of oranges and purples. It was so beautiful the way the colors touched the mountains. I thought of the thousand sunsets I had seen living at the ocean; a lifetime in living color. There had been so many good times. Wonderful sunny days filled with volleyball and swimming. Daddy had been in the center of it all, laughing and joking.

Donna, there you go again. You don't seem to focus on the problem here. Your father is evil. What do I have to do to remind your? E. V. I. L. Must I really spell it out? He would have hurt your Julie. How easily you forget about Keely and the lips.

I know. I know. But this is so hard. I don't want to be brave.

You are brave. You always were. Have I ever let you down? Wasn't I there with you all those years when you felt hopeless? When you wanted to walk into the ocean and never come out? Didn't I promise you...Just because you have been feeling better doesn't mean anything has changed.

March 1990
Spring Break
Mammoth Lakes

Ken and I were enjoying a vacation at Mammoth. My mood swings between terror, guilt, and sadness had leveled off. My nightmares were subsiding; my dreams frequent and clear.

I could hear my dad's voice in my sleep. One night he said "Donnie, you should not be doing this." Then the voice was gone. Another night I dreamed that a young mother had come to a two-story house with a circular staircase. She was in a waiting room, waiting to have my father babysit her little girl. I could hear myself interfering; felt my familiar knot of terror. I told her not to allow him to stay with the child.

She said, "Thank you." She did not know me, but she said, "I believe I remember that he molested me when I was little." With that she had gathered up her child and left. The other dreams had me waking up in pools of blood, my teeth falling out, being chased, locked out or running. They were horrible.

One night Ken answered a call from Cee Cee. I could tell from the way he was trying to calm her, the way he asked her to repeat herself that she was hysterical, probably crying and choking. I felt panicky just hearing one side of the conversation. After 20 minutes Ken hung up.

"Cee Cee has discovered that your dad did hire a detective. Some woman visited your friends, the Moores, unannounced. She just surprised them at dinner time, got herself inside their house by posing as a representative of the court, an impartial investigator. She led them through some interesting verbal acrobatics before it became clear that she was investigating you." Ken paused.

I felt my face go pale. I was the innocent party. Why should I be investigated? The Moores had been family friends for 30 years. They were my parents' age, but I had kept up the contact between us with Christmas cards and letters. They knew me well.

"Well, two hours later, after ruining their dinner, the detective left. They told her that the frame-up charges against you are bogus. The Moores went on to explain that you had many times greater net worth than your father. They told her that you were a woman of the highest character, a college professor who had been teaching at the same school for a quarter of a century. And that they trusted you beyond any doubt. They told her that they had even owned property with you for years. I don't think from what Cee Cee said that the detective got what she came for. At the end of their interview, they had volunteered that your father's treatment of Connie was 'very peculiar and overly affectionate.' They also said that whatever Donna said had to be true."

"So why exactly is Cee Cee so upset, Kenny? It sounds like Dad is really just coming after me, like he always said he would." My heart was thumping. "She was frantic, wasn't she? She seemed to be from what I could hear."

"Oh, yes, she's upset all right! The detective next grilled Bernie for two hours. It was another surprise visit. Bernie won't take sides. Cee Cee is furious with her. She can't understand why her mother won't help her with this. And she's worried about your father's threats to obtain a court order to seize her therapy records. She thinks he will try to prove her to be a nut case."

"I think therapy records are confidential," I offered calmly, fighting to think clearly.

"Donna, it makes me so damned angry to see you girls frightened like this. You are being manipulated by these meaningless threats. No court in the land is going to subpoena therapy records. If they did, big deal, they would show the depth of Cee Cee's abuse at your father's hand. I'd really like to kill the bastard."

Quivers of fear threatened to break loose. For Ken, I tried to keep myself together. I had come this far. I didn't want to lose it now. I tied up those fears again with steel cables.

"Donna, let's get outside for a while. How about walking up to the ski lodge and back? You look like you could use some night air?"

As we walked, I sorted out the pieces to my puzzle

"Ken this is kind of off the wall, but do you remember Crystal's paternity suit against Dad?"

"Oh, yeah!" His words were tinged with laughter. "You don't forget something like that. It was pretty strange when your dad married her. Didn't he say he married her because he was afraid she'd kill him?"

"Yes. That seemed silly until their bizarre divorce. You know I bought Dad's story that she trashed his house, flooded it, sprayed graffiti on the walls and sold all of his furniture because she was nuts. But I think it was something else."

"What do you mean?" asked Ken.

"All these years I thought that her paternity suit against Dad was strange. It cost him $60,000 to beat it. I never really got why she did that. And then when the genetic testing results proved that her little boy could not have been Dad's, I thought she was as crazy as Dad said she was. He was always saying that she was very dangerous." I pondered their relationship for a moment. "You know, I always wondered what triggered such venom on her part."

As we walked on in the night, I considered it more fully.

"Ken, she must have caught him with Jaime. Jaime was about five when Dad took them in. Wrecking his house, the paternity suit...Ken, it was her way of getting even. It was the only way she could get back at him." I paused and reflected. "I bet dad's detectives were able to dig up enough dirt to discredit her."

"I bet you're right! Her actions don't sound crazy if she was getting even with him for molesting Jaime!"

We silently held hands as we strolled up the hill to the ski lodge, a three-story concrete colossus quietly bathed in moonlight. The skiers were gone for now. Ken and I climbed up an incline, snowless now as the ski season was almost over. He led me to a clearing under a pine's full skirt. Sheltered by the fragrant branches, he pulled me close. "Donna," he spoke softly, "this will all be okay. Look out there."

The mountains were serene under the stars. Ken and I embraced, and I remembered the years of good times with my family.

Once when Danny was six, he talked me into going up on the chairlift with him during a blizzard. I was a raw beginner. My poles were askew and my skis crossed at the last second, after he worked so hard at getting me into my seat; so hard that he fell off his chair. The lift was stopped and the operator scolded me for not getting Danny on his chair correctly. When we got to the top of the hill, we were laughing so hard we practically collapsed into the snowbank.

"Mommy, he thought you knew how!" Danny, the excellent skier, doubled over at the thought of his mom, "the klutz," being competent.

"Just wait, Danny. Someday I'll beat you down the mountain." It was such a farfetched claim we both rolled our eyes skyward.

Yes, I reminded myself, there had been so many wonderful times. I don't know how I would have made it through this time of terror without my solid base of family love.

Slightly chilled from the cold night air, we hiked back home, hand in hand. I felt much better. Joy warmed me. Serenity calmed me. The fear had lifted for now.

I held my anxiety in check during the remainder of the week, but by the last morning of our vacation, as I cleaned up the kitchen counters in preparation for our journey home, the steel cables holding my icy block of fear in harness began to slip. I continued wiping. My breathing became shallow. I was losing control. The demons of fear locked away in that steel chamber near my soul were climbing out. The last cable broke, and they tumbled forth.

Ken heard my choking cry and came to me at the kitchen counter. He surrounded me with his strong arms as I sobbed and sobbed.

When he thought I could talk, he asked solemnly, "Donna, what's wrong?" He was patient and understanding.

I tried to say something but it came out only a choked garble. I felt ashamed; I had always prided myself on my control. I could handle anything, but here I was, so pathetic that I could not even talk.

Kenny pressed a kiss into my palm. He tried again, "Donna, can you tell me what's wrong?" There was a very long silence. I suppose he thought I had not heard him, but I was trying to sort out what was so troubling.

Finally, much later, I answered, as we headed down Interstate 395 on our way back home.

"I'm just so afraid he's going to *get* me." It finally spilled out. Kenny reached for my hand. There was no talking for a long time.

"Sweetheart," soothed my husband, "He won't get you. He cannot hurt you ever again. He is locked away in jail. Why are you still afraid?"

"Kenny," I took in a deep breath. "I broke my contract."

"Sweetheart, what contract?"

"I told." I began to cry again. "I promised that I never would."

"Donna." His right arm came behind the seat and he pulled me against his side. "You were only a little girl. No adult in the world has the right to involve a young child in such a contract. You didn't even know what you were promising."

"I promised never to tell." My words broke off again.

"Donna, you were a little kid. You didn't even know how bad it was going to get when you promised. You had to break your promise, Sweetheart." Ken raised his voice. "Sweetheart, you had to tell!"

"He always said he'd get me if I told. And I told." The sobs wracked my body as we headed toward home. It was a blessed release.

May 1, 1990
San Juan Capistrano

    This morning, as I drove the 37 miles to my college, I heard my favorite broadcaster on 104.3 FM wishing us a happy May Day. Of course, I remembered that May Day long ago in second grade. I still remembered the looks on the other children's faces as they stared at the warts on my hands. I would probably always remember.

    I slowly made my way north past the Irvine Ranch. Cows grazed on the dried spring grass close to the road. The 405 freeway was clogged with traffic. I had a lot of time to think.

    I thought about our upcoming court date. Tomorrow we would have to take the stand after months of postponements. The prosecutor was hoping to get a plea bargain from Dad in order not to traumatize Keely by putting her on the stand, but all this waiting had produced nothing.

    It would be the preliminary trial in front of a new court. Tightness choked my throat. I felt strangled. I swallowed and took one of those big deep breaths my therapist had harped on me to use.

    "Breathe, Donna," I said aloud in the privacy of my car.

    Seated in the comfort of my motionless vehicle, I thought back to a night when Cee Cee had called me, desperate for help. I had been asleep, but the ringing phone finally awakened me. I stumbled out to the kitchen and played the message. She sounded terrible.

    I woke my sleeping husband. "Kenny, it was from Cee Cee!" The fear in my voice brought him fully awake. I punched in her number. It rang once.

    "Oh, Donna, thank you for calling me back. I'm sorry it's so late. I didn't know what else to do.

"What's wrong?" I hoped that I sounded calm.

"It's Keely. She had another one of those nightmares. She woke up screaming and then stopped breathing like that time in Phoenix at Thanksgiving," Cee Cee's words raced out.

"When she stops breathing and turns all blue, her lips go purple, and I think what would I do if I didn't have my Keely anymore."

"Cee Cee, Keely's okay, isn't she?"

"Yes, when I couldn't get you, I yelled at her to breathe like you told me. That seemed to startle her and she coughed and took a breath. She's back to sleep. I just don't know what to do anymore." Her voice sounded detached, past desperation.

"Cee Cee, we're all doing our best. You are doing well. Keeping everyone together right now takes everything you have. This will pass in time. We have to be patient." I hoped that I sounded reassuring. I was fighting my own demons. I tried to believe my own words.

A horn blasted, jolting me suddenly back to the present. The cars on the freeway had begun to inch forward again and a huge space loomed in front of me. I eased my foot off the brake, closing in the traffic gap.

As the traffic let up, the line of cars accelerated to 25 miles per hour. "The Boss" was shouting out *Born In The USA* from the radio. I started to enjoy the beat of the music. Somehow this song resonated with me and I felt stronger as I continued on to work.

Deep inside, I felt steel tumblers turn and fall into some unknown and precise sequence and that familiar wall of strength fell into place like a steel partition. I felt solid, secure. My gentle inner voice reminded me:

Donna, you are doing the right thing. You must protect the children.

May 2, 1990
Municipal Court Building
West Los Angeles

Ken and I walked up the wide cement steps in front of the West Los Angeles Courthouse to await the preliminary hearing for my father. The court would decide today if there was "just cause" to try him in Superior Court.

My father had now been in the Los Angeles County Jail on a "no bail" status for more than three months. Using the pay telephone, he had continued to run a successful reign of terror from his cell. Cee Cee and I were ragged from his jailhouse threats which came to us via Connie, Trey, and the hired caseworkers and private detectives who were probing everywhere, asking questions about us.

Today was trial day. Ken opened the huge double glass doors for me as we entered the foyer of the court building. Far to the right, huddled on a wooden bench in front of Division 91, sat Cee Cee, a tiny woman, looking fragile and younger than her almost 40 years. She was dressed in an attractive blue business suit trimmed with white lapels; her long dark hair was pulled back. There was no evidence of the hip, heavy metal seductress.

As I drew closer I could see her face. It was pale and her body language read, "Near hysteria." Next to her sat Anne. She was smaller than her mother at 4 foot 11 and maybe weighed 100 pounds.

Anne greeted me with a sad silent look as she got up to walk toward me for a hug. She was dressed perfectly in a tailored navy blue dress. There was a bit more color in her pale cheeks than in her mother's, but not much.

On the other side of Cee Cee sat Keely, precious in a blue and white pinafore. Her black, silken hair was combed long down her back. Evenly trimmed bangs framed her delicate features. She looked like a miniature Snow White. Immaculate. I always marveled at how clean and well-dressed Cee Cee kept her children. Keely and I enjoyed a bear hug for an extra moment.

"Aunt Donna, say 'Hi' to my bunny."

"Hi, Mr. Bunny."

"I told you the bunny was going to talk," she stated in her high little voice.

"You sure did, Keely!" I smiled. I hoped my voice sounded okay.

Ken had learned that the district attorney would only call Cee Cee, Anne, Jesse and Keely to the stand. I felt relief that today would not be a repeat of January for me. I knew that my day would come again, however, if this case made trial. For now, though, we were all restricted from the courtroom.

We were very concerned about Keely. We could not predict how all of this would affect her or how she would react in the courtroom. Would she testify? She had not said one word on the stand during the "trial run" the week before. She had been afraid of the lady in the black coat.

Late in the afternoon Keely was finally called by the bailiff. I watched her through a small rectangular window in the door. She was dwarfed by the adult-sized courtroom. The floppy beige bunny, ears askew, was tucked under her left arm as she raised her right hand and spoke the oath which I had repeated months before from the exact spot. I had been scared then. Keely must be terrified now.

"Do you solemnly swear to tell the truth, the whole truth, and nothing but the truth?"

I knew the words, and could see Keely saying yes. She then walked confidently to the stand. She looked so tiny standing there, next to the witness stand railing. She was only slightly taller than the partition which separated the gallery from the trial area.

Keely walked around to the witness stand, climbed up the step, and pulled herself up onto the seat. I could see her head bobbing up and down. She was speaking with animation. The beige bunny was in her arms, but she was doing the talking. She had warned me again before she went into the courtroom, "If I get really scared, the bunny's going to do the talking, but I'll be the bunny's voice!"

So far the bunny was mute. I could not see them from my vantage point at the door, but I knew that her feet in their lacy socks and black patent leather Mary Janes did not reach the floor. I wondered how there could be a culture in which little children are molested, abused, and then forced to sit not ten feet from their abusers and tell the sordid details so they can attempt to achieve safety through a complex legal system. I dreaded the scars this might embed in her memory.

Daddy could have stopped it. He could have pled guilty. He could have gotten six years, three on parole. That would have been a good deal for him. But Dad would not budge. He was a gambler. This time the stakes were his freedom.

After a long while Keely came out. She seemed pale, but okay. Later we learned that Dad kept waving cheerfully to her, trying for her attention, to the point that the bailiff had to come over and tell him to stop or have his right hand cuffed.

Still barred from the courtroom, I stood next to the crack in the door and looked at dad while the judge rendered her decision. The case would be sent up to the Superior Court.

I was frozen in fascination watching Dad. He was dressed in the blue cotton coveralls that he had worn previously. They were emblazoned with Los Angeles County Jail across the back in black letters. The flesh on his once huge biceps hung limp. I stared as the bailiff slowly unlocked his left hand which was handcuffed to the chair and brought his right arm around to join his wrists behind him. In that second, Dad flung out his arm in violent defiance, a mini show of what hid beneath his friendly exterior.

In the next moment Dad stood and walked slowly away, escorted by the bailiff. He fell back into his pathetic prisoner role, displaying his arthritic limp. Why was he limping? His hip surgery and subsequent therapy last year had gone beautifully. Did he really think he could evoke sympathy?

May 16, 1990
Rose's Office
Newport Beach

I was tired of all this therapy, sick of not feeling happy.

"Rose, how much longer before I am well? As you know I'm very patient, but I don't have much time!" I looked down at my watch to emphasize the shortness of time. I liked my little joke. My mood lifted a little.

"I just don't know," Rose spoke seriously. "It takes people different lengths of time. Slowly the good days will string together and you will feel a bit better for a little while longer. You are experiencing grief. Grief is at the core of delayed stress syndrome. You are grieving over the death of your 'fantasy father,' the loss of the contact you have had with your real father and your lost childhood."

"Rose, it has almost been a year and I still only get a day or two off from feeling upset."

"I know. It will get better. You were never allowed to be a child, Donna. You've been a little adult since you were two-years-old and Sandy was born. You acted as a little parent to your baby sister and to your own parents. You were required to keep an adult secret and to understand adult issues. You were robbed of your childhood. You must grieve that loss before you will be better."

On my way home, I thought of my father. Daddy always wanted me to be perfect, to be good, to be honorable, to be strong and to be his star child. Could some part of him have helped to shape me into someone who would stop him? I grappled with that ultimate irony. Perhaps Daddy built in his own nemesis.

May 22, 1990
San Juan Capistrano

"Donna?" inquired a low voice. It was the district attorney working on our case.

"Yes?" I pulled the telephone tighter against my ear.

"Is Ken there? I've been paging him for two days."

"No." I began to feel wary. "He's moving Rick from law school. He'll be gone all week."

"Donna, I didn't want to call you before this," he stumbled hesitantly. "I...I didn't want to upset your weekend."

As he spoke, the adrenaline began to speed through my veins. My stomach constricted. I knew bad news was on the way.

"Something went wrong last Friday at the Superior Court arraignment. I thought the new judge would rubber stamp the Municipal Court judge's decision but..." he paused again to let that news sink in. "But, Donna, are you safe?"

Yeah, sure! I thought, gripping the phone.

"As of five o'clock this afternoon, your father had not yet been released from County Jail. Once the court directs a bail, there is no system in the district attorney's office or in the police department for monitoring when bail is made. Donna, you could know when he makes bail before we do!"

"What should I do?"

"If you have any problem, call 911 and a SWAT team will be there in minutes. We're not going to let anything happen to you. Tell the 911 operator that you are involved in a case with detective James Bowen of the Los Angeles Police Department. His name will signal the SWAT team status. The police are on standby. You'll be okay." He was trying to bolster me. It was not working.

The district attorney's voice grew more serious. I knew that he was genuinely worried about me, about us. He cared about this case. I strained to listen to his every word of direction.

"Donna, he might explode into violence. I don't know...Just don't forget. If there is a problem, dial 911. They are only a phone call away!" He was trying to sound reassuring as he ended the conversation.

"A phone call away!" I thought quietly. I was completely alone in my home except for my two dogs. My husband was going to be out of town all week.

I locked every possible access. I knew I had truly put my life on the line. I knew that if Dad were released, I was in big trouble. I recalled Dad's threats. Somehow they weren't enough to deter me. I had come to a new plateau in my personal development. The threat to my safety was less important than protecting Keely.

I felt like some mad fool loose on Maslow's last hierarchy, self actualization. A professor friend once told me that if you get to Maslow's highest level, no one can have power over you because you have moved beyond their sphere of influence.

So much for philosophy. I didn't feel as if I had self-actualized or reached my potential as a human being. I just felt scared.

May 30, 1990
Emergency Bail Review
Superior Court Building
Santa Monica

Today was our fourth court appearance since Dad's arrest in January. Dad had not made bail yet, and Ken had persuaded the prosecutor to appeal the low bail. We had another chance.

The legal proceedings usually moved faster, but the law took its time when children were involved. They were still trying to spare Keely the agony of testifying. The defense had requested two continuances during these past five months and we had asked for one during the week of our brother Chad's wedding and honeymoon.

The district attorney had gone in person to the jail to offer a last plea bargain of only six years, three years of actual time if Dad would plead guilty. Dad refused again. He would not admit his guilt.

Tentatively, I opened the door to courtroom number 208. It was almost empty. The judge gestured for me to come inside.

"Is it all right?" I asked hesitantly. He smiled and assured me that it was. I waved to my family and we filed into the small wood-paneled courtroom. As we took our seats the judge, a handsome man in his late forties, leaned back comfortably in his heavily upholstered chair and spoke to us. It surprised me. The other judge had been unapproachable.

"Are you all here to observe?"

"No," I answered. "I wish we were. We have business before you today." He looked at me with more interest, his expression asked what business. I responded, "The Ray Landis case." He checked his calendar and nodded his head in agreement.

"We've had a circus here today," he said in an engaging voice, inviting conversation. He then proceeded to share some of the day's anecdotes with us. He was relaxed and charming, and I found myself breathing easier. I unclenched my fists.

Soon my father's defense attorney entered and took a seat near the jury box to wait for the hearing to begin. The district attorney entered the courtroom and joined him. The two men chatted quietly as we waited. They seemed friendly. The bailiff, a nice-looking black man, entered and both attorneys took places at the long walnut table facing the judge at the front of the room. We were told to leave. The proceedings were about to begin.

Through the two small panels of glass in the double doors of the courtroom, I could see the bailiff bringing in the prisoner. I was getting used to seeing Dad with grey hair now. A month before, at the preliminary hearing I had been shocked to see that his blonde hair had turned grey since he could no longer color it. It hung longish and unkempt over the collar of his blue coveralls. He had lost weight.

Nora, the case worker from Stuart House, came to the courtroom door and asked me to come in. My heart was pounding, but I took another deep breath and walked in.

I knew that I looked every bit of what I was: a college professor, a poised strong woman, a successful mother of three accomplished adult children. I was a woman up to fighting to protect the children, who finally had come to understand that she herself was worth standing up for. A woman who had somehow moved beyond the fears for her own safety, who could go into battle if she were forced to.

The court clerk asked me to raise my right hand and to swear to tell the truth. I did so. I walked the three steps and stepped up to the witness stand which was to the left of the judge. I adjusted the microphone and breathed slowly, deeply. I avoided looking to my right, to where my father was sitting next to his attorney at the mahogany table.

The questions began. The district attorney asked my name, age and relationship to the defendant. I answered confidently, slowly spelling out my last name, clearly articulating my age. My voice was disciplined.

"Have you ever been molested by this man?"

"Yes, since first grade when he took me to school. He accomplished rape when I was nine-years-old in our trailer at Sycamore Cove above Malibu."

"Do you feel in personal danger?"

"I was always told that 'people who talked end up six feet under.' Yes, I feel in personal danger," I couldn't keep the anger out of my voice.

"Have you ever personally been threatened?"

I lifted the single sheet of paper I held in my right hand.

"I received this reply back from the last letter I sent my father. It's a poem. I'm not sure what it means. Perhaps it is a threat on my own children's lives. I'm not sure."

"Would you please read the poem?" The judge asked kindly.

I read it aloud in my best speech-teacher voice.

"The troops, nearly always innocent of the nature of war, march boldly forth…Other innocents, at home…" I stressed the phrase 'innocents, at home.' " I let my voice make the nuance. I completed the poem and looked at the judge.

"Has the defense seen this?" he asked. I sat quietly.

"I believe so, Your Honor," replied the defense attorney.

"May I see it again?"

With that the bailiff approached me and took the paper. As the moments passed, the judge spoke to me in a low voice.

"This is just routine. Don't let any of this bother you. You are doing fine." He was soothing. I felt better, not too scared. The questions continued.

"What effect would the prisoner's release on bail have on Keely?"

"She would be severely affected. I have had two past-midnight phone calls during recent months from her mother. Both times Keely stopped breathing in the middle of the night. She was having a nightmare each time. In one of her nightmares Grandpa was coming to steal her. In the other, Grandpa was under the bed and he was going to get her."

The courtroom was silent. Everyone waited for me to continue. I reached back in my memory to find what I had said to Keely. Her mother had put the phone up to her ear. I began again.

"I said to her, 'Breathe, Keely. It's Aunt Donna, Breathe, Keely. It's okay. Grandpa isn't going to get you. You are okay now, Honey. Breathe, Keely.' There was no response. I didn't know what else to do. I was frightened. I shouted at her, 'Breathe, Keely!' After a bit she cried out and took a breath. Her mom came back on the phone."

I paused for a moment, all eyes on me. "Your Honor, Keely also attempted suicide. She said, 'I'm going away soon.' She meant that she was going to drown herself during one of her privacy baths. We found her 'practicing' with a tub full of water."

"No more questions," the district attorney concluded.

The defense attorney rose to question me. He stood right next to my father. I would not risk looking in his direction. I did not have the strength to look at Dad.

The defense established that I frequently chatted with my father on the telephone. The sound of the defense attorney's voice seemed to imply that if I talked to my father, he could not be guilty of the charges.

"I talked to my father several times a week, four or five times, until I got so bad last summer that I couldn't talk to him anymore. I wrote him a letter and explained that I was very upset. "

The defense attorney avoided following up that line of questions. He seemed to avoid any discussion of my mental health. Trying a new line of interrogation he asked. "Isn't it true that your father sent you through college?"

Obviously the defensive position was to prove what a good guy Dad was. I could not believe what a platform they were giving me.

"No, it is not true."

I carefully recited my educational degrees and honors and described my nearly full-ride scholarship. I even got to say that I was currently enrolled in a Ph.D. program. Perhaps Dad had led this attorney to believe that he had paid for all my education or maybe he had even convinced himself. Who knew?

Dad was always saying that Bernice had put Sandy through dental school. What a lie. Our mother and aunt had loaned her the money. It had taken her years to repay them.

"Have you ever known your father not to show up for a court appearance?"

"I find it difficult to equate tenant evictions with raping your own little girl," I responded in a controlled, slightly sarcastic voice. "No, Dad never missed his day in court if a tenant owed him money."

"Have you ever known your father to own a gun?"

"Yes, always."

"Were these guns ever anywhere other than at his home?"

"Yes, on the boat," I replied.

"Did you ever see him shoot anyone with them?"

"No."

The judge turned to me. "You may step down."

Six of us testified. After our testimony the judge looked right at Dad and said, "Mr. Landis, you are a dangerous pedophile and a threat to society. Bail is set at $500,000."

After it was over, we all met on the steps of the Santa Monica Courthouse. We were relieved for the moment, but we still needed to be together for a little while. We sat in a circle on the grass. We planned Cee Cee's birthday party next month at our house. Afterward Ken took me out to dinner and a Goldie Hawn movie. I laughed all the way through it and he held me close.

As we drove the hour home to San Juan Capistrano, I leaned back against the upholstered seat of Ken's oversized truck. Resting my head on his shoulder, I put the courtroom and the past out of my mind. I looked out of the window. We were coming on the south end of Orange County where four new multi-storied glass buildings had recently arisen out of the strawberry fields. We had witnessed an incredible amount of development during our 25 years here. Our home had once been in the country. The original Juaneno Indian Tribe had lived on our land, and our children had found an Indian arrowhead in our yard after a heavy rain. I felt deeply rooted, connected to this land.

A new strength was asserting itself in my center. I felt okay now. Maybe even better than okay.

June 15, 1990
San Juan Capistrano

I made my way out to the kitchen. Warm air rushed into the room from the open windows. Summer was definitely here.

Rosa, our housekeeper, was busily collecting plastic cups and party remnants from Cee Cee's fortieth birthday party the day before. I poured myself a cup of coffee and admired my china cup. I had painted my dogs' faces on it.

The party had been special. We enjoyed the pool and had lots of good food, and Ken had taken the kids on horse rides. Cee Cee had even made a speech. Surrounded by a brightly colored stack of gifts, she had begun in a soft voice.

"I've had one of those grins all day that won't go away. Everyone knew that my sister was having a birthday party for me today. My first!" She smiled.

This was a new Cee Cee, a more confident happy woman. At least having Dad in jail all these months had helped her to find herself. And what a delightful self she had found. Her face glowed with love and excitement.

"When I was a little girl, I spent a lot of time thinking. When I was in the closet hiding, which was often, I would dream that a day would come when people would really know me. When I did not have to pretend anymore. Well, that day has come. Thanks to Donna for breaking me out. For stopping it."

With those words, she smiled warmly at me and our eyes met. She told me more in her look than her words could ever express. She was thanking me for her life. *Dear God, I did not mean to be responsible for anyone's life. I just knew that I had to stop him.* I tried to tune back to Cee Cee's words, but my inner voice reminded me gently:

Donna, evil can only flourish where people do nothing to stop it.

Yes, I believed those words, but why me?

Why not you, indeed? Exactly you, Donna. Exactly you.

I heard Cee Cee as she continued, "And I want to thank Sandy, who had the courage to confront him and for helping me to find my courage." She then searched the room and her blue eyes stopped at Kenny.

"And I especially want to thank Ken who has held me together all these months. If it had not been for Ken, I never would have made it. He is the only man that I have trusted for a very, very long time." She smiled warmly at Ken. "I want to thank you all. This is the most wonderful day of my life. I feel so loved by everyone."

We had a wonderful birthday celebration. Cee Cee's friend from childhood, Michelle, even joined us. Michelle was thrilled to be reunited with Cee Cee after almost 25 years. It was strange the way Michelle had suddenly come back into our lives.

Six weeks before, Michelle had been awakened from a dream about our family at exactly 2:30 in the morning. She thought it was odd because she had not had any contact with us for two decades. When the dream persisted, she had to get in touch with us. She found Sandy's phone number in the book, called and explained the odd awakenings.

Sandy immediately replied, "Michelle, our dad is in jail. He had been molesting Cee Cee's little daughter."

"Oh no," she muttered. "He did that to me when I was little. I was so young I didn't know what a condom was. He taught me. It took me five years of psychotherapy and shock treatments to get better."

When Sandy relayed this to me, I plunged into a terrible despair. I fell to the floor in the kitchen in a ball and keened. I hurt to think that those who had been our friends had not been safe. I clearly remembered picking Michelle up from fifth grade when I picked up Cee Cee. She had been a skinny little girl with a long blond pony tail. Others had not been safe. It was almost more than I could bear.

July 2, 1990
San Juan Capistrano

Alone on my patio I lay in a lounge chair, eyes closed. I pulled my sun hat across my face. I tried to turn my mind off, hoping to rest. The Fourth of July would be quiet this year as it came on a Wednesday. There would not be the usual big weekend with our friend Patty and her family.

We had enjoyed 15 years of volleyball weekends with them competing over a little trophy that moved from one mantel to the other. I smiled at that thought. The warm sun beat against my skin, still cool from working inside. My thoughts moved back to the last court appearance, the bail review on May 30, Superior Court.

Ken and I had arrived early to wait for Cee Cee, and I'd remembered another time I had waited for her. It was such a clear memory it might have been last week. Cee Cee was two- years-old and I was nine. I could still see her in minute detail. She had twin pony tails and bangs. Her dark hair was cut to just above her deep blue eyes. I was happy it was her birthday.

Two-years-old. I could still see her racing up the sidewalk in front of Big Ray's drug store, her chubby little legs carrying her as fast as they could toward my arms so that I would twirl her around. A shiny #2 button was pinned to her green dress. She was a big girl now.

I pulled her into the familiar swing she loved. As I lifted her, I could feel the soreness. Every muscle in my body ached. I could barely move fast enough to get the right momentum. It took everything I had. I moved my feet in their familiar circular pattern, and spun her around as best I could. My sister loved the twirling, but I had to stop. I just could not continue, the pain was too much. I still remembered Cee Cee's puzzled look.

"Donna, Donna, more! More, Donna!" She had demanded.

I tried to divert her attention. I knew I could not continue to swing her. Just walking was painful. "I have something for your birthday." I smiled, putting on my cheeriest voice. "It's a big surprise!"

"What? What?" She was curious at once. She wanted her birthday present.

I set Cee Cee down very gently and straightened up slowly. We went inside the drug store then to get Cee Cee her present.

That was the morning after Daddy had taken me to Sycamore Cove to fish. I caught a shark. He told me I was a *real woman*. Oh dear god...............

Cee Cee's birthday always reminded me of that terrible trip. That memory was a difficult one to put to rest.

July 3, 1990
Rose's Office
Newport Beach

Seated in my favorite spot on the corner of Rose's soft leather couch, I began to talk. I felt miserable.

"So, Rose, why do you think my father did these things?" I stopped to think for a moment. "I know this is odd, but discovering that he molested other little girls, little girls outside the family, somehow seems even more horrendous to me. I'm not sure why, but it really does bother me. Something deep inside me feels responsible for his hurting them. I just don't understand it."

"Donna," Rose responded thoughtfully, "studies show that most sex offenders were molested themselves as children. So, as adults, many re-enact that same abuse. Maybe it makes them feel superior to overpower a helpless child. Maybe it is about their own rage. Some researchers think that the offender identifies with the victim. We don't really know. These are just theories. It may be that they are most stimulated sexually by recreating their original abuse."

I shared a dream I had just had that morning. In it we all visited Dad in jail. He had gifts for us. He was at Terminal Island Federal Prison and his cell had an ocean view. He wasn't angry at any of us.

Rose just sat quietly and let me describe the dream. She listened intently as I continued.

"You know, the psychological literature is full of the term 'magical thinking.' That is what kids do to make things better. It occurs to me that perhaps this magical thinking actually takes place in the unconscious where there are no conscious controls, and then somehow spills over into our consciousness and becomes thoughts. My dream magically gave me Dad's forgiveness," I stopped to think for a moment.

"It is really an issue with me," I paused. "Though I try to push it down, it is really an issue that Dad is angry with me." The thought hung in the air for a long while.

"Let's get back to your earlier question. Why is your father a child molester?" Rose brought our focus back to my original concern. "We know how homophobic your father is. I suspect that it was your grandfather…"

My grandfather? What had he done to Dad?

It would be some time before I thought to study my grandmother's journal of her trip around-the-world taken when my father was only five-years-old. Family lore had it that my father never again called her "mother" after that trip, only "Maymie." That trip, I knew, had been a cruel turning point in his young life. The journal entries described a ragtag child who was so angry with his mother that he refused to come into the house and greet her after the three-month-long trip. He had been in the care of his father and also his uncle. I would always wonder what happened during those months when my grandmother was away.

September 8, 1990
San Juan Capistrano

We were in and out of court many times. We lost the rape charges brought by Cee Cee and two of the girls. The district attorney told us that too much time passed for Anne and Diedre's charges to be valid. California has a six-year statute of limitations. I reacted with shock when told the reason that Cee Cee's rape charges would not hold.

"Let me get this straight," I asked the district attorney. "You mean that because Dad was not holding a knife to Cee Cee's jugular, it is not considered rape? She was afraid that he would kill her son, Jesse, because of what he'd witnessed. Are you telling me that's not menace and duress?" My tone was harsh. Where was the fairness in this law? What about the rights of victims?

"That's what I'm telling you. The law doesn't provide for this kind of rape."

The molestation charges on Keely would remain, and Cee Cee could at least charge Dad with incest. The trial was scheduled for the end of September. It was difficult to settle down and live life with such desperately unfinished business. It had been almost a year since our battle had begun and still it was not settled.

I thought of a Bible quotation that my friend Sharon had sent me. The words from *Luke* comforted me greatly: *"To the one whom much is given, much is required."* I knew that there was truth to this quotation. I had been given so much good as well as bad. I thought of the trial and how much was required.

Another quotation came to mind. Trey's fiancé, Shelby, had asked me to do a reading at their wedding. She had chosen something from *Corinthians:* *"Love takes no pleasure in other people's sins but delights in the truth. It is always ready to excuse, to trust, to hope and to endure whatever comes. Love does not come to an end."*

I had dedicated my life to that idea, been sorely tested by it, and yet continued to believe it with all my heart. I felt this love glowing in my heart, content, tender, and hopeful. I thought of my beautiful grown children, my loving husband, my friends, my extended family, and my students. So many to love. So much to look forward to.

October 22, 1990
San Juan Capistrano

"Hello," I answered the phone on the third ring. It was Monday evening.

"Aunt Donna?" asked a little girl's voice.

"Hi, Keely. How are you, big girl?"

"Aunt Donna, um, I, um…I'm working on my birthday list. My birthday is Thursday."

"I know, Keely! I sent you a box full of surprises. You'll get it soon!"

"Aunt Donna. Anne was here. First, I asked Mommy for a trip to Jamaica. Then I asked Anne. They both told me to call you, Aunt Donna. I want to go to Jamaica for my birthday."

"Jamaica?" I laughed. "You silly. What's this about? Wait, first tell me what else you might want."

"The ballerina doll. She dances and has pretty clothes and an outfit just like my Halloween outfit. She has a little ruffled pink dancing skirt. Anne said she was getting that for me."

My warmest laughter filled the distance between us. "Keely, I don't think the trip to Jamaica is going to work out, but I put some neat stuff in the birthday box I just sent you!"

"You did? What?" she asked excitedly.

The diversion I hoped for had worked. "Well, just watch for the UPS man. He'll be there soon."

"Aunt Donna, would you and Uncle Kenny come to my birthday party on Saturday?"

"You bet. We'd love to. Why not put your mom on and I'll find out what I can bring. I love you, Keely."

"Okay. I love you."

"Donna," Cee Cee laughed, "I didn't know what to do with her trip-to-Jamaica plans. I thought you might. I have no idea where that came from!"

"Thanks a lot! Hey, I just let it go right on by. She is so funny. You and Anne get off with a doll and I'm stuck with the travel plans!" We were both laughing now.

It was so nice for us all to be laughing again. The defense attorney was still arranging for delays, and the prosecution cooperated in hopes of a plea bargain. We all knew it wouldn't happen. Dad would never admit anything. But for the time being he was safely locked away and we could relax.

November 3, 1990
The Beach
Dana Point Harbor

This morning I packed my textbooks in a bag with a bathing suit, suntan lotions and a yogurt lunch. Now on sabbatical leave from my teaching position, I was a full-time student with lots of homework. I was excited about my doctoral work. I had waited many years for this and finally it was my turn to go back to school.

Fifteen minutes later, I settled myself into my beach chair on the warm sand. A school of porpoises greeted me from offshore, swimming in close. The peculiar southern current which had warmed our waters all summer was still with us. It had delighted us with exotic species of fish.

The days were shorter now, and tinged with autumn coolness, but it was still a California beach day. Textbook open on my lap, I looked past the porpoises to the distant outline of Catalina Island resting peacefully on the horizon. Ken and I had spent whole summers there with our little ones. Julie, Rick and I had collected shells and made necklaces out of them.

We had enjoyed a lifetime of family pleasure. Many such happy memories included my father. Today was his 67th birthday. I hadn't forgotten. I envisioned him with his latest toy, an air buoy. It was an air compressor attached to hoses and masks, a kind of scuba system. He loved that crazy thing.

With his trial approaching in just ten days, my ocean-view prison cell dream was recurring. In one dream, Dad even had presents for us when we visited. He wasn't angry. He said he was fine and he smiled at me. Then I woke up to realize that it was all just a dream. Ugly reality washed over me. Nothing was okay.

Last week Dad subpoenaed Keely's and Cee Cee's therapy records, trying to prove that Cee Cee is mentally disturbed. No, nothing is all right.

These thoughts of Dad brought me despair. I searched my consciousness for something more peaceful, and my mind turned to my marriage. There were some difficult years, financially and emotionally. No marriage of 26 years was all smooth sailing. The truth through it all was that Ken and I never lost our faith that two people, two bad risks for marriage, coming from troubled and broken homes, could make a marriage work.

Sometimes we white-knuckled it as we went along. I suspected that Ken had been doing this all year, holding me and my siblings together during this awful time. He'd also had to deal with the disillusionment of not having been allowed into my private world. Although he hadn't known me as he thought, Ken stuck by me when many men would have run away.

As the heat from the sun danced over me, my heart did a little race and my lips moved instinctively to a full smile. I probably looked like a dope, lying on the beach in late autumn, smiling like a moonstruck young girl. I knew that I had something precious with Ken. He was my friend, my lover, my soul mate. I would always be grateful for that.

December 20, 1990
Superior Court Building
Santa Monica

The trial finally started, five weeks late. It was 8:50 in the morning, on a California day that was crisp and chilly.

Ken and I were posted outside the courthouse searching the traffic for signs of Cee Cee. She was late and we were getting nervous. She was supposed to take the stand in half an hour and still needed to go over her testimony with the district attorney, Bill Peters. We'd all been wrecks for weeks. This made it worse

"Cee Cee has been so punctual all week," said Ken peering down the street for any sign of her blue van.

"I know. They're starting with her at 9:30." I was worried, too.

By 9:30, Ken and I were really unnerved. Ken left me to go inside and tell the District Attorney that his witness wasn't here yet. Minutes later, I spotted Cee Cee across the courthouse lawn. Rand had let her out of the van while he searched for a place to park. Rand had been wonderful through this ordeal, supportive and loving toward all of us.

"Cee Cee!" I called. "Over here!"

"Donna!" She yelled, hurrying over toward me. "I was so bummed this morning. Just getting all the kids up, dressed and organized to be here this early is bad enough but then there was an accident on the freeway. The traffic on the 405 just stopped. I tried not to wig out. I just told myself that they could always slip another case in front of ours."

We hurried into the courthouse and took seats in the waiting room of the prosecutor's office. Ken came in and reported that the judge had given us a half-hour delay. Cee Cee began to dig around in her large handbag for the transcripts of her conversation with Dad. She had about 60 pages to work from and was to be questioned on the last two conversations this morning.

Dad had succeeded in removing the judge who had heard the bail review from the case. He claimed that the judge was prejudiced against him. It had added months to the trial process. We were all very frustrated, especially Bill, the district attorney. The new judge had imposed severe constraints on the case

The district attorney complained to us that he was boxed in. During the first two weeks of trial, the new judge ruled that a major portion of the evidence was inadmissible. No mention of the histories of the noncharge victims could be entered. None of Dad's photographs of partially nude children, which had been used at the preliminary hearing, could be entered. There could be no actual playing of the taped telephone conversations with Dad, and possibly not even any testimony from Cee Cee's and Keely's therapist.

In fact, Bill reported, if any of us so much as uttered a sound of our own abuse in front of the jury, it would result in a mistrial. He cautioned us time and time again to be very careful about what we said in the courtroom. It was absolutely clear that we should not tell much at all. For days we all had been very angry about the heavy prohibitions.

This judge had a reputation for being very tough on both defenders and prosecutors; consequently his cases were seldom reversed during an appeals process. I have since learned that 95 percent of all Superior Court cases go through the appeals process. I was getting a crash course in how concerned our system was about protecting the accused.

Until proven guilty, Dad was considered innocent and his rights were protected. Not only had he been allowed to change judges, but he now had a special van bringing him to and from jail to the courthouse. He claimed the regular prison bus got him back to jail too late and it interfered with his sleep. Ten of the initial 15 counts against Dad had also been dropped because of technicalities. He had definitely scored some serious victories

We were all critically aware that the district attorney had promised us no easy victory and that juries can go either way. He said "beyond a reasonable doubt" actually means "absolutely without a doubt" to the jury when it comes to their verdicts.

I was coming to believe that the guilty have the advantage. Certainly in this case, Dad did. The deck was clearly stacked against us. The burden of proof lay completely on us, which meant that it ultimately rested on the words of a scared little six-year-old girl. When I thought of what Keely was being put through, what we were all being put through, my anger flared to the surface.

The reality of going up against someone like my father, of actually trying to get him to stop molesting our family, was unimaginable. No wonder I had never seriously tried in the past. As far back as elementary school I had known that I needed power. I had always known that without power, I would be dominated forever. As I grew older, I realized that the key to my freedom lay in education.

I turned my head and observed our newly selected jury forming a line in front of the door to our courtroom. There were 16 of them, ordinary, nice-looking human beings. Four were alternates. Emotion went through my body like a 7.4 earthquake. It seemed deplorable that we had to have these strangers help us stop our father from molesting. It was all so pathetic.

No one before now had ever had the power to stop Dad. No one had ever been able to stop him from doing exactly as he pleased. What would these 16 people do?

Would we be able to stop him? I understood the possibilities that Dad could be set free. A shiver shot through me as I tallied what had been involved all along. First you have to deal with your own abuse, figure out how to admit that it happened. Come out of the comfortable cocoon of denial, confront the issue, the shame and the risk of Dad's wrath. Then you had to convince the social worker and the police that you had a problem. Then you had to put together a case, wait a year, have the judge rule that Cee Cee's charges under California law did not qualify as rape and that Diedre and Anne's counts exceeded the six-year statute of limitations. It all seemed so unfair.

The judge had also ruled that Keely's therapist could not testify regarding Keely's behavior or any conversations she'd had with Keely. It had been a terrible blow to the prosecution. The D.A. was furious. We were all furious.

"Good morning, Donna," Los Angeles Police Detective Jim Bowen greeted me as I entered the room. He had worked tirelessly on our case.

"Donna!" Cee Cee turned from her work at the long walnut table. "Bill wants me find out where we left off in court yesterday afternoon and rewrite the lines that are left. Remember the judge won't admit any line that refers to any other girls. We can only use references to Keely." Cee Cee leafed through a stack of pages. "We got about halfway through yesterday."

I sat beside her. "Bill said that when he took his position as D.A., he took an oath in which he promised to find the 'truth' in his cases. This is such a monumental irony that should any of us slip up while we are on the stand and let a little of the real truth be shown to the jury, we'll end up with a mistrial."

Suddenly Cee Cee stood in her sailor-style suit, ridicule playing across her pretty face. She raised her right hand in a parody of an oath.

"I hereby promise to tell just the teeny-weeny slice of the truth that you will allow, Your Honor, so help me, God. I understand that under no circumstances do we want to find out all of the truth. Amen." She chuckled, enjoying the moment of comic relief.

"Your Honor," I mimicked, feeling my anger dissolve as I raised my own right hand, "I hereby promise not to let the jury know what really happened, lest they think that Dad is really not such a good guy. We surely do not want the whole truth to slip out. I promise, so help me, God."

We both smiled mischievously. Perhaps gallows humor was better than no humor at all. Our eyes met in merriment and lingered affectionately. I knew we were a study in what sisterhood was all about. Glancing at the clock, I noticed that we had only two more minutes. Bill Peters and Jim Bowen walked through the office area.

"Ready, ladies? We're on," said Bill, sounding relaxed. The afternoon before, he had been mostly smiles having finally convinced the judge to allow Keely's therapist to testify. He thought our case might still have a chance. Bill looked much more confident now. His youthful grin had returned.

As we headed toward the courtroom, I scanned the last pages of the telephone transcripts. Over and over again Cee Cee had brought the conversation back to sexual abuse. Over and over again, Dad had dodged it. She had done a brilliant job of coming back to the point. Perhaps Cee Cee should have been an attorney.

We all gathered around Cee Cee, flanking her. Rand, Ken, my mother, Bill, Jim and I marched down the hall, past Bernie and Connie. Bernie had not spoken to Cee Cee all week. A family divided. Those two were on Dad's side.

December 26, 1990
Superior Court Building
Santa Monica

The presentation of evidence ended today. The defense simply rested. They presented no case. The entire burden had been on the State. The judge spent the morning admonishing the jury regarding procedure and law. The jury then left for the day. We had only to wait for the verdict which we expected in the morning.

It had been a very hard few weeks. The final awful week in which 13 of us testified against our dad had probably been the worst. All those long weeks leading up to it were plagued by never-ending continuances. Dad's demand for a new judge took the longest time because it meant that our case had to trail behind another case.

We had been in limbo for three weeks, with no certain date for our case to begin. On the day it finally was to begin, the prosecutor charged Dad with two more counts against Keely. There were more continuances by the defense. It had dragged on for what seemed like an eternity.

At last our day in court came. Keely arrived upstairs to be the first witness for the State. She was nervous. Her six-year-old little hand was hot and sweaty in mine. She was wiggly and upset easily. Her anxiety was palpable.

Finally the bailiff gently called, "Keely Kelly." She reluctantly left my embrace and walked through the double doors of Department F. She was a very little girl in a very grown-up battle. That thought tormented me. How can we have a system that sends a tiny person in all alone to testify against a big strong adult sitting only a few feet away from her? Why is our society so reluctant to believe that this goes on? Why are there so many hurdles? I wanted to scream my indignation out.

Keely testified for the rest of that day and for most of the next. Those were long difficult days, but we made it through them, all of them. The detective and the district attorney both said that Keely was the best child-victim witness they had ever seen. I hoped that this experience would pass quickly into a blurry and foggy memory for her.

During my testimony I was numb. It amazed me that I did not feel much. Somehow I had detached myself and I was even able to look at Dad. He didn't look like my dad, though. The father of my dreams was laughing, young and funny. This man was old and angry, as he attentively listened to my answers, his jaw muscles working furiously.

The details of my testimony were devastating. It was enough to render anyone who loves children emotionally incapacitated. I hadn't let it do that to me, however, I remained semi-detached, mostly in control. My iron reserve protected me. Cee Cee's strength grew during the many days we spent in court. It was truly a test of our mettle. Now we just had to wait for the jury to make a decision.

"Donna? How are you holding up?" Ken asked as we walked from the courthouse to our hotel across the street.

"Average. Shifting gears from our nice Christmas yesterday back to this mess is pretty difficult."

"Do you want to take a nap this afternoon?"

"No," I shook my head. "What I really want to do is rent bikes and ride down the beach on the bike path. I want to see the place where I grew up. To see if I'm okay."

It all happened in such close proximity, the wonderful and painful events of my childhood, and our terrifying effort to bring my father to justice. We could almost see the beach where I grew up from the courthouse steps. I need to close the circle. No matter what the jury decided about the fate of my father, I needed to connect with my childhood again, to try to lay the demons to rest.

We found a place to rent bikes, and Ken and I pedaled our way south along Santa Monica Bay toward Venice. My spirits began to lift as we followed the sand-strewn bike path past the scenes of my youth, and pleasant memories flooded in. There was the restored Hippodrome Carousel building at the entrance to Santa Monica Pier. Nearby, I saw the place where Big Ray used to play checkers. All through my childhood in the late 1940s and early 1950s, Sandy and I would find him there.

I could remember paying my nickel to ride the tram north, from the Ocean Park Pier to the Santa Monica Pier, to look for Big Ray. Sandy and I would always find him at one of those tables, intent on his checker game. All the players on the beachfront called him Doc. They said he was one of the best in the state, a champion player.

Ken and I pedaled slowly, past a sign announcing, "Original Site of Muscle Beach." Forty years ago, in the span between the Ocean Park and Santa Monica piers, private beach clubs attracted the affluent while the amusement piers attracted families. Thousands and thousands of people thronged to this area yearly. It was the "in" place.

Now it was empty on this winter day. We rode along the cement strand and I pictured it as I had known it as a child. The benches along the sidewalk had been occupied by hundreds of short, thick-bodied European refugees, speaking their own native dialects. I had marveled at the many layers of dark clothing they wore, even when it was hot. The women had dark scarves covering their heads. As a child, I did not understand the terrible fates they had barely escaped in Hitler's Germany. I had not yet seen the stretcher-shaped crematoria in Aushwitz. Those refugees were gone now, their progeny, no doubt, well-integrated into the life of Southern California.

We rode past a stand selling T-shirts declaring "Muscle Beach," "Venice" and "California" on their fronts. A Hyatt hotel was under construction next to the old Del Mar Club. The club had become Synanon in the early 60s, a drug rehab house before its time.

We rode on. I couldn't be sure just where the old Ocean Park Pier had been. The landmarks had all changed. I searched for any sign of it. I could almost hear the din of the crowd along the boardwalk, could almost feel the calliope music and the excitement of the carnival rides.

Riding the carousel, I had loved it when I actually got the brass ring. It was a cinch to reach my right hand up and grab at the rack holding the rings. I always tried to pick the white horse with the black tail and fierce jeweled eyes. He seemed to rise higher than the others so that I never missed my ring. I rode and rode for hours while Big Ray played his "last" game of checkers.

My husband and I pedaled slowly, enjoying the sound of the gently breaking waves and the smell of the salt air. I could still remember the audacious cackling of those big fat ladies. They were only wooden dummies, laughing hysterically as they tried to lure us into the dark mysteries of their fun house. I could taste the vanilla custard. The stand was decorated like the North Pole with penguins and icebergs. Dad would buy me the custard, an early version of a frosty. It always had a cherry on top and it tasted so creamy and yummy. He would pay for it and hand it down to me smiling.

"Here's a sweet for my sweetest girl."

"I love you, Daddy."

Ken and I were entering the Venice area now and pedestrian traffic picked up. There were so many tourists. Affluent Asians, old people sitting in the sun, black youths trying to look tough. A melting pot. A colorful mosaic. I loved the diversity of Southern California.

I craned my neck to look down Windward Avenue. A few of the colonnades still remained from the early Venice days. I remembered the shoe store next to what used to be a Bank of America. Bernie took me to buy my first pair of school shoes there. Now it was just an empty lot. We were almost at the entrance of the old demolished Venice Pier.

"Ken let's walk our bikes!" I yelled over the noise. "I want to see what's going on. Why do you think that crowd has gathered?"

"There's a limbo dancer in there somewhere." He paused, waiting for me to catch up to him.

"Kenny," I whispered, "See that man?" I nodded toward the tall, turbaned man on rollerblades. "I've noticed him for years. I want to have him play a song for me. He has the most incredible blue eyes." I felt excited, happy. "Want to come with me?" I urged.

"Ah...no, I'll just watch," he refused with a smile.

A few minutes later, I bounced cheerfully back to my husband. "It was a dollar a song. Did you hear it?"

"Yes, I did. So what's his name?"

"Would you believe Karma Kosmic Krusader? He's probably really Wilfred Green from Detroit," I added. We both laughed. "He says that he has been skating and playing his guitar along here since 1974."

"Only in Venice," my husband responded with a little smile.

"Now I want to go into the little building over there." I pointed to the tiny cement office where my mom had supervised the playground 42 years before. I noted that the current play equipment was much fancier than it had been back then.

The girl's bathroom was the same, but seemed much smaller to me now. Water pipes were still visible against the wood-sided walls. The red cement floor still had a fine layer of sand.

We remounted our bikes and continued slowly, visiting my first elementary school. The alley next to it, where I waited for Sandy to get out of kindergarten, was the same. We visited the remains of the canal bridge, near where I caught guppies. Now million-dollar homes graced the waters. We passed the Edgewater Market Building, which had become a realty company. I remembered reaching for Sandy's five-year-old hand as we stood in front of that big store ready to cross busy Washington Boulevard.

"Donna, maybe we should go another way. It's only a few more minutes to your dad's house. I'm not sure this is such a good idea."

"I need to do this. If I'm not okay, we'll turn and go on Pacific Avenue."

Pedaling at a comfortable pace, we soon came to my father's home. Over 4,000 square feet of beach-front structure, it stood three stories tall. We stopped our bikes in front. It looked the same except the new owners had changed the color. I looked across the sand to the sea and felt the rhythmic pulse of the waves breaking. The ocean was a constant in my life, comforting me.

"Are you sure you're okay with this?" Ken asked, worriedly examining my face.

"Yes," I answered, still very much preoccupied with the past.

I opened the gate and looked for names carved into the cement. Leanne, Donna, Sandy. We were always laying cement and carving our names in it. But now there weren't any names. The patio floor had been covered over with Mexican tile.

Not much of us was left. There was no hint that we had been there, struggling to build the foundation forms. No clue that two young girls moved yard upon yard of sand from the front of the lot to the back, no clue to reveal that a father and two daughters had removed the foundation pilings from this site with a hand-held jackhammer.

I realized suddenly that I was letting go. The pain that I had pushed back for so many years was being exorcized. I knew that I would be all right. There would be no more dark secrets, no more night terrors about Keely. There would be no more pretending to be okay. From now on, it would be true.

Exploring the scenes of my childhood was an impromptu ritual, moving me from within my safe little chrysalis into a butterfly. I could imagine butterfly wings, brightly colored in blue and white, spreading open, allowing me to fly into my future. A great weight was lifting from my shoulders. The days of anxiety would soon be over.

I knew I had come full circle. I had reclaimed my childhood and was free to move on.

January 3, 1991
Superior Court Building
Santa Monica

    The jury was still out. We had been certain that the verdict would come in by late the Friday before. Surely, the jurors did not want to interfere with their long New Year's weekend as they had with their Christmas holiday? Again, we had been wrong. By 5:00 on Friday afternoon there was still no verdict.

    We suffered through the long weekend, returning on the first business day of the New Year, certain there would be a verdict. No such luck. Today, we were again hopeful for an end to our long vigil.

    The district attorney, Bill Peters, came in as he did frequently to speak to our family. "Wow, your ranks have grown!" He smiled noticing the increase in the size of our group. Bill turned to Cee Cee and spoke very seriously, "I wanted you to know that as of January 1st, two days ago, menace and duress are grounds for rape charges in the state of California." He nodded, handing her a thick document. "Because of you, Cee Cee, we managed to get a law changed, and that is extremely difficult to do. Never again will a judge be able to discard rape charges because they were based only on threats to the victim. If it's any consolation, the injustice you suffered may not happen to anyone else."

    Cee Cee leaned against the wall with a wide smile. Pride gleamed in her eyes. "That's pretty good, huh? At least something positive will come out of all of this." Her voice filled with emotion. A state law had been changed because of our case. We all felt that something significant had been accomplished. Our battle had been worth it.

At last, at 3:30 in the afternoon we were ushered in to the courtroom. The verdict was in. Ken and my sons determinedly took the front row of spectator seats, instinctively moving to protect me. Rick, now an attorney, wore a grim expression. Dan's strong young warrior face showed his determination. Tears stung my eyes. It occurred to me that I had borne and raised my own private militia led by Ken.

Julie took a seat next to me in the second row. She reached gently for my palm and held it reassuringly between her strong hands. Ken reached behind his seat and found my right hand. Chad, sitting next to me on the right, put his arm around me. Leanne sat close by, keeping a silent vigil should I need her. It hurt in a peculiar way to finally have a safe place. My husband, my sons, my daughter, my adult brothers, my family and friends would protect me.

There was a stirring in the courtroom as they brought Dad in through the prisoner's door. He looked strong and angry, dressed in a beige corduroy sports coats and handcuffs. He studied us carefully for a long two minutes before he took his seat. In a loud, tinny timbre, much higher than his usual voice he spoke to his attorney.

"Well, there are my little *darlings!*"

We were always in trouble when we heard *"little darlings."* The sarcasm, however, was lost in the oddly elevated pitch. His words no longer instilled fear. How peculiar! My breathing became easier.

The jury was brought in and they took their seats quietly. The judge began immediately.

"Mr. Foreman, has the jury reached a verdict?"

"Yes, Your Honor," answered a heavy-set man in a dark suit.

A slip of paper was passed to the judge, and then handed to the court clerk. The court clerk stood.

"Your Honor, the jury finds the defendant guilty of two counts of lewd and lascivious conduct with a child, guilty of one count of oral copulation with a child and guilty of the charge of incest. The jury could not reach a verdict on the fifth count.

At that point, the judge rasped in a fierce voice, "The court finds the defendant guilty on four counts. The defendant has broken the sacred trust of a grandfather caring for a small child. Sentencing will be February 1, 1991."

Oral copulation! Oh no, I thought. Emotion once again seized me. It was terrible enough to know what Daddy was, but to hear it out loud was even more terrible. Julie clutched me tighter. Ken gently stroked the top of my hand with his thumb.

The jury was excused. As the bailiff handcuffed Dad and took him away, he glared defiantly at us. I turned my head to look at Cee Cee. Tears streamed down her face. She, too, was in the throes of emotion, caught between what was left of her love for Daddy and what he had done to her little girl, to all of us little girls.

We filed quietly out of the courtroom. Cee Cee and I embraced, our tears mixed together on our already wet cheeks. We had come so far in our struggle. Neither of us dared to trust our voices. Sandy embraced us both. She was dry-eyed, tough and triumphant.

"I've been waiting 30 years for this! This is the best day of my life!" Her voice was exuberant.

My children came to me then, one by one. Rick silently held me to his strong chest. Dan stood by patiently and then when his brother released me, he enclosed me in his arms. Beautiful tenderhearted Julie stayed close by my side, watching me for any cues that I might falter. Leanne, too, a few feet away, kept a close watch over me.

Finally there was Ken, waiting for me, standing quietly by. Dear, sweet Ken. I shuffled into his arms. He wrapped me in his embrace. We stood there for a very long time in the late afternoon shadows of the courthouse hall. For all of our ups and downs over the years, he was always there for me. Ken had led the charge in a most ghastly war and we'd won. He had supported me and guided me in our battle.

My gentle inner voice reminded me.

To protect Keely.

To protect the children...

Epilogue 1991

My father was sentenced to the maximum term allowable by California law on March 8, 1991, a term of 12 years and 8 months in state prison. During his sentencing, the judge said that my father was worse than the mass murderer Charles Manson and wished that the laws allowed his sentence to be a thousand years.

As of January 1, 1991, California state law was changed to include menace and duress as grounds for rape charges. This was a direct result of the court case against my father. Never again will a judge be able to discard rape charges because they were based only on threats to the victim as happened to Cee Cee.

Epilogue 1997

August 6, 1997
San Juan Capistrano, California

Tonight my father died of leukemia, alone, in a prison hospital room. He was to be released in just five weeks. I am sad tonight as I write this for what he could have been with his advantages, his handsome good looks, his creative intellect and his wonderful sense of humor. He could have been anything at all. Sadly, my grandmother's old prophecy still rings in my head, "I am afraid that Junior will end up a penniless old man alone in a room somewhere." How right she was, and how very tragic that is. It feels awful to me that 20 years ago she could see into the future. Clearly, he was always on a collision course with his destiny. Each time he reached for any of us girls, as toddlers, children, pre-teens, and teens, he pulled himself closer to his eventual destruction. It hurts to recall that a few times he confided in me that he felt a sense of quiet desperation about his life. I shudder to think what it means to possess so many of God's gifts and yet to know of your own silent hopelessness. It is unimaginable to me that a person could see catastrophe on the horizon and yet fail to change its inevitable course!

I understand that he threw away the deep love of his many children because his need to satisfy his depraved cravings was more important than any other single force in his existence. I know that in the days to come I will shed tears for the daddy I loved so much and pretended to have, and for that misled man that he became.

A few weeks ago a whole group of us went as a family to Disneyland. It was a warm summer evening full of laughter and love. Quietly watching Disney's Magic Light show, leaning against Ken, encircled by his strong arms, I looked at the kaleidoscope of lights playing across the sky and my thoughts turned to Daddy. I had so wished on that night that things could have been different. I felt a terrible twinge of regret as the bright colors danced across the heavens that he was not there with us, glorying in all of his beautiful children, grandchildren and great-grandchildren.

I smiled as I thought of the jokes he would crack and the funny antics he would play. He could be so delightful. I know that my thoughts turned to him because he was always taking us to Disneyland when we were young. He loved life and he especially adored his children and that magical theme park. But on that night, he wasn't there with us. He would never be there with us again because of his willful choices. He would never meet Julie's two beautiful young children. He wouldn't see two-year-old Jake's golden red hair and huge hazel-colored eyes, nor hug Rick's two darling little girls, two-year-old Jillian with her giggles and white blonde hair, and sweet little Megan. He would never look into their great dark blue eyes and see his own genes reflected back at him. How terrible that because of his choices he would never laugh with any of the other wonderful children recently born to his children and grandchildren.

It made me very sad that evening as it does tonight. I stayed present in that feeling for a long while. I was used to it. The tender, loving little girl inside of me often looks upon a star on a clear Southern California night and wishes that her daddy could see it. It has been terribly painful knowing that that his life in a cell had doubtlessly prohibited him from enjoying a starry evening.

As always I forced myself away from those gloomy thoughts. I reminded myself that he had repeatedly been offered plea bargains, which would have had him released five years ago. Then I thought about those letters. All those long letters in his precise engineer's block print. For eight years we had received pages of threatening words. His ramblings repeated time and again that God would punish us, that we had violated his commandment to honor thy father, that I was a traitor and should "be dead." His letters were ghastly missives filled with ranting to justify incest, that it was God's will.

It had been a difficult eight years as we moved on with our lives and tried to heal from our childhood devastation. We had been doing pretty well, even our sister Connie who continued to have a relationship with Dad, talking to him each week on the telephone, was married and had two children and ran a successful day care business. Since the trial, I have worked to sort out my life and gain some perspective. I have come to understand that for most of us, the life we are living is a result of our own personal decisions. Our decision as a family was to protect Keely and our other little girls who had not yet come into the world. We had made a decision to stop the abuse and now that it is over, I see that we are beginning to triumph over the tragedy of Daddy's actions.

Recently, I have devoted my energies to becoming a voice against sexual predators. Last year, I was honored by President Bill Clinton and the United States Department of Justice for my advocacy work. I have been honored to be present with California Governor Pete Wilson at three different bill signings; bills to help protect the children. As for Ken and me, our marriage is strong, our children are flourishing, we have our health and we are moving forward into the light.

Suggested Reading

Bateson, Mary Catherine. **Composing A Life.** New York: Atlantic Monthly Press, 1989.

Bateson, Mary Catherine. **Composing a Further Life.** New York: Alfred Knopf, 2010.

Berne, Eric. **What Do You Say After You Say Hello?** New York; Bantam, 1972.

Blume, E. Sue. **Secret Survivors: Uncovering Incest and Its After Effects In Women.** New York: Wiley and Sons, 1989.

Bradshaw, John. **Bradshaw On: The Family.** Deerfield Beach, Florida. Health Communications, 1988.

Bradshaw, John. **Healing The Shame That Binds You.** Deerfield Beach, Florida. Health Communications, 1989.

Canfield, Jack. **The Success Principles.** New York: Harper Resource Book, 2005.

Cleckley, Hervey, M.D. **The Mask of Sanity**. New York: Bloom Book, New American Library Mosby, 1982

Covey. Stephen R. **The 7 Habits of Highly Effective People.** New York: Free Press, 1989, 2004.

Covey, Stephen. **First Things First.** New York: Fireside Book Simon & Schuster. 1994.

Csikszentmihalyi, Mihaly. **Flow: The Psychology of Optimal Experience.** New York: Harper and Row, 1990.

Ennew, Judith. **The Sexual Exploitation Of Children.** Oxford: Polity Press, 1989.

Frankl, Viktor. **The Will to Meaning.** New York: Meridian Book. 1966, 1989.

Friess, Donna, L. **Circle of Love: Guide to Successful Relationships, 3rd Edition.** California: H.I.H. Publishing, 2008.

Finkelhor, David. **Sexually Victimized Children.** New York: The Free Press, 1979.

Fortune, Marie M. **Sexual Violence: The Unmentionable Sin.** New York: The Pilgrim Press, 1983.

Forward, Susan. **Toxic Parents.** New York: Bantam Books, 1989.

Gallagher, B.J. **The Power of Positive Doing.** Illinois, Simple Truths, LLC, 2012.

Gil, Elianna. **Treatment Of Adult Survivors.** California: Launch Press, 1988.

Goleman, Daniel. **Social Intelligence.** New York: Bantam Book, 2006

Masson, Jeffrey M. **The Assault On Truth: Freud's Suppression Of The Seduction Theory.** New York: Farrar, Straus and Giroux, 1984.

May, Rollo. **Love And Will.** New York: Norton, 1966.

Miller, Alice. **The Drama Of The Gifted Child.** New York: Harper and Row, 1981.

Miller, Alice. **Thou Shall Not Be Aware: Society's Betrayal Of The Child.** New York: Harper and Row, 1981.

O'Kelly, Eugene. **Chasing Daylight: How My Forthcoming Death Transformed my Life.** New York: McGraw Hill. 2008.

Peck, M. Scott, M.D. **People Of The Lie: The Hope For Healing Human Evil.** New York: Simon & Schuster, 1983.

Rock, David. **Quiet Leadership.** New York: Harper, 2006.

Rock, David. **Your Brain at Work: Strategies for overcoming Distraction, Regaining Focus, and Working Smarter All Day Long.** New York: Harper Business, 2009.

Rush, Florence. **The Best Kept Secret: Sexual Abuse Of Children.** New Jersey: Prentice-Hall, 1980.

Shengold, Leonard. **Soul Murder: The Effects Of Childhood Abuse And Deprivation.** New York: Fawcett Columbine, 1988.

Steiner, Claude. **Scripts People Live.** New York: Bantam, 1974.

Thomas, T. **Surviving With Serenity: Daily Meditations For Incest Survivors.** Deerfield Beach, Florida: Health Communications, 1990.

Tillich, Paul. **The Courage To Be.** New York: Yale University Press, 1980.

Woolf, Virginia. **A Room Of One's Own.** New York: Harvest: HBJ, 1929.

Cherish the Light: Breaking Free
of the Dark

Donna L. Friess, Ph.D.

The sequel to *Cry the Darkness*

PROLOGUE

August 15, 2012
Boardwalk
Santa Cruz, CA

"Mimi you want a leg up?" asked my strapping 17-year-old grandson, Jake, as he boosted me onto the carousel horse of my choice. It was a shiny white beauty mounted strategically on the outside lane, all the better for grabbing the brass ring! A wave of pleasure pulsed through me as I admired her ruby eyes. She reminded me of my pony, Pixie, at home, and of course, of the long ago favorite carousel horse when I was a child. This was so much fun! I was glad that I had flown up to Oakland to meet up with Julie and her boys to check out universities with Jake.

"Jake, great. I'm set!" I was up and readied myself to grasp the rings as we whirled by. James and Julie were on the horses in front of me and Jake was just behind. We were lined up as sentries determined to get those rings, all of us sporting eager smiles. I snapped a few photos and secured the camera around my neck. The organ music started up and our horses began to move, slowly at first, but gaining speed with each rotation. We could hear the clacking of the rings as they loaded into the delivery shaft. We were off!

I watched as Julie successfully plucked her first ring, then James who missed his, and then it was my turn. Out went my determined fingers, but I missed. Around we went again, gaining more speed. Julie yanked and then tossed her ring at the waiting clown's face. Next was James, successful this time, and jubilant. Then my turn and I grabbed it. I was so elated that I forgot to toss it at the clown! Around and around we went, faster and faster. I managed to nab a ring and then toss it. I was heady with triumph, so much so that I was barely ready when my turn came again. I missed. This time Julie managed to get her ring into the much smaller target of the clown's open mouth. A victory! Julie bellowed out her joyous success.

Whirling and grabbing, smiling and laughing, around we went and with each cycle my brain spun backward to my 7-year-old arm stretching out as far as possible, ready to clasp the same kind of ring. It was the Ocean Park Pier of my childhood. The 1940's, still the heyday of the waterfront amusement piers located up and down the west coast. In full view of my memory, I could almost smell the cotton candy and hear the delighted squeals of the children mixed with the canned laughter of the two Laffing Sals, who welcomed guests to the famous seaside park. Sandy would be behind me frantic to grab a ring. We rode the merry-go-round so often in those days that catching the coveted brass ring and getting a free ride were frequent, yet much sought after, events.

Perhaps I was reliving a Sunday of my childhood. Sandy and I would have walked from the tiny beach cottage where we lived to Muscle Beach in Venice. I was probably holding her hand to keep her safe. I would have paid the five cents it cost each of us to ride the tram from Venice to Ocean Park where we would have checked in with our checker-playing champion grandfather, Big Ray. He would have looked up and smiled his toothless grin, introduced us to his fellow checker players, reached into his dark suit pocket and retrieved some coins for us. There would have been a hug exchanged and then Sandy and I would have scampered off, free to ride the carousel for the next few hours. The checker players would have gone back to trying to beat "Doc" at his game. In those days, he was famous in the checker playing set of Los Angeles.

Smiling for that sweet memory, I came back to the present moment, not so different from those of 60 years ago, but now I was the grandparent and the children were my grandchildren, but I was not playing checkers, I was still after that brass ring!

I smiled to myself, surely I had won it. It had to be the brass ring to raise such a beautiful healthy family and decades later to be playing the same kinds of amusements with them that I had so enjoyed as a child. The Long Beach Pike, Ocean Park Pier, Santa Monica Pier, Santa Cruz Boardwalk, Playland in San Francisco; what delicious memories! Hot blueberry pie in San Francisco after Sandy and I had rolled and rolled in the tumbling tunnel of the fun house, delectable frozen "cream" at the Arctic ice cream parlor in another, adrenaline charged whoops on all the roller coasters up and down the coast; those fun zones had a magic of their own.

The trademark of that bygone era, before Walt Disney got his big idea, had to be those iconic Laffing Sals. From 1930-1950 three hundred of them welcomed guests across the country. The stout animated feminine figures sported a gap tooth smile, giggled and gyrated to attract in patrons long before the Disney animatronics characters were born. I remember that the raucous cackling from those two Sals at Ocean Park was all it took to turn on my own giggle machine. I could not walk past them without breaking up in my own delighted squeals. Just thinking about it still cracks me up, they never stopped; they just laughed and laughed and laughed!

I love that the Santa Cruz Boardwalk exhibits one of the very last Sals in existence. In a way, it feels like visiting a piece of my own past. The Sals have not been seen much since the 1950's. The fun zone beach parks have mostly disappeared across time, victims of storm damage and social change, but this one in Santa Cruz boasts that it is the only one on the whole of the west coast that has been in continuous operation. Today, it has two gigantic roller coasters, arcades, aerial trams, whirly rides and of course bumper cars.

The bell clanged and the carousel slowed down and came to a stop. As we climbed off our horses, Julie looking cute in blond pig tails, animatedly recounted her victorious toss into the clown's actual mouth, Jake proudly reported that he caught a ring on each turn, and James smiled as he said, "So Mom, I am ready for that dessert now. I am thinking ice cream dots."

"Not until I get you guys at bumper cars!" challenged Jake.

"I'm up for it!" I chimed in.

Bumper cars! I feared that my dear Jake was in for a jolt to his "world view" regarding his Mimi, me. My wonderful boy had no idea when he challenged us and climbed into his shiny blue bumper car what was in store for him. The starting buzzer sounded and the electric floor became "hot." I could see Jake in front of me a few cars up. I slipped around a green car, gained speed and WHAM! I quickly crashed into the back of him. Shocked, he turned around to see that it was me, his gleeful grandmother, laughing like a maniac, as I raced away to the safety at the perimeter of the floor.

I turned for a quick glimpse and saw that he was in hot pursuit. I swerved between a few little kids in slower cars and kept to the edge. Jake's face was all determination as he gunned it. He was coming for me, but suddenly the congestion in front of him forced him to slow down. I made a quick get-away! I kept my wits about me and slipped between the colorful cars until I was behind him yet again. Wham! You could almost see him thinking, "What? Not again!" Our family is nothing if not competitive. With an even more resolute set to his shoulders, he took off in full pursuit, but by now I was way in front of him. Around and around the floor we chased each other. I could tell that he really wanted to get a shot at me, but I was too slippery. I am sure he was thinking that there is no way this grandmother is going to get the best of me! I kept to the edges of the floor and then like a stealthful guerilla warrior I emerged from the cover of the other cars to strike him yet again! He tried his hardest to reciprocate but I was too fast and too sneaky. The ending clang sounded. Ha Ha! My childhood strategy of cruising the periphery until my target was within range paid off.

During all that zooming around that electric floor, an old memory came to me about how much Dad had loved the bumping cars. Actually, he had been quite a devotee of all such amusements and by our teens my sister Sandy and I, with our Dad leading the charge, had visited all the major such attractions in the United States on our various treks across the country with camping trailer in tow. They were good memories; happy memories. It was always best for me to stay in that mental place.

As we concluded our visit and continued down the boardwalk, Julie linked her arm affectionately around Jake's neck. James put his arm around my waist as Jake summed up the afternoon, "Well, Mims, I had no idea that you had a secret life as a commando. That was some fancy car bumping. Lady, there is NO way this is over! There is going to be a rematch and watch out! I'm going to devote my full energies to practicing so I can whomp you next time!" teased Jake, his light green eyes dancing with merriment.

"Hey, so who is ready to head south and explore Big Sur?" asked Jake. "During the drive here, while the Mimster was obviously scheming about bumping cars, I found a really awesome waterfall in the California guide book. I think we should hike to it. It is 75 feet tall and the fresh water cascades onto the beach!"

With that we were off on another part of our adventure and I knew that I was enjoying the best adventure of all, sharing these precious moments of this check-out-the- universities-road trip with my daughter and grandsons.

As Julie's SUV headed south on Highway 1, my memory kept coming back to that delightful amusement pier. In a way, I grew up around them. I had loved the Ocean Park Pier, which was right by our house. I remembered that in the late 1950's it was sold and became Pacific Ocean Park. It was very popular while I was in high school, and then somehow over the years while I was raising my family it was boarded up and eventually torn down and I never thought much about it.

That image brought me to another memory of another boarded up pier. When I was a kid, a beautiful pier stood at the end of Venice Boulevard from 1921-1946. The Red Car was a street car that deposited thousands of eager beachgoers to the foot of the Venice Pier all summer long. It ran from downtown L.A. to the beach. When I was a young child that pier still stood; closed-up but still present and situated next to the playground where our mother was a recreation leader. I have dozens of photographs of my great-grandparents and my grandmother Maymie posing in front of it. It had always intrigued me as in some ways it seemed to contain a mythical ghostly vibe of my long ago ancestors, but during my days it was but an ancient relic.

Suddenly, a long ago memory transported me to a hot summer day. Our mother was tending the playground where she worked not 100 yards from that pier. Sandy and I had the job of keeping out of the way. On this particular day, an older girl with a nervous little dog dared Sandy and me to go into the closed-down pier.

"We're not supposed to leave the playground." I responded in a worried voice.

"Well we'll just be gone for a minute. Your mom won't even know you're gone. She's busy with that carom tournament. Come on! Or are you a yellow chicken?"

Not one to easily back down, I agreed to go, but just to look. Taking Sandy by the hand, we sneaked up the ramp into the pier and slid in between two loose boards. It was spooky. It was so dark down below that you could barely see the white foam of the waves, but the moans of the surf crashing into the pilings were eerie. One false step and certain death lay below.

We traveled a little further out onto the pier. We must have been inside some kind of old structure, maybe an old fun house. The malignant moans of the waves continued; crashing and receding. Suddenly the older girl raced across the single plank, stretched precariously over a wide space. I took her dare, but soon realized it was a bad decision. My child's terrified voice still rang in my memory as I yelled to Sandy, "Stay back. This is scary. Sandy, stay back!"

I imagined what could have happened had I fallen into the dark waters below. What if Sandy had followed me across? She was so little. I remember that we raced out of there and ran back to the safety of our corner of the sand box. We stayed there for a long time, each of us lost in our own thoughts. Later, our mom came looking for us. We never told her about our terrible adventure. It was our dangerous little secret.

From the back seat Jake handed me the guide book as he said, "So Mimi, here is that picture of the falls I want us to see."

With that, I turned my attention back to the present. As I leafed through the pages of the guide book, I thought how lucky I was to be traveling with the kids like this, to be a part of this giant-sized family and to be enjoying the past mixed with the present. I understood that my choices had led me here to this moment, and this life, but it could all have gone so horribly wrong. One missed step and as dad always said, "Sorry sisters end up six-feet-under." I refused to go to the place where I thought about what scars must have been left deep within my psyche, the residue from years of living under my father's reign of terror.

I thought about my new life; all the kids, my wonderful husband, my beloved Golden Retrievers, my life coaching practice and the grief counseling work I did. Ever since *Cry the Darkness* came out 20 years ago, readers have badgered me to know the secrets of how I have succeeded in having a happy life. Even today, my clients continue to ask, "Donna explain how you have managed not to live as a victim? How do you stay so focused on the positive in life? You are the most joyful and positive person we know. How have you done it?"

How indeed? A good question.